Helion & Company Limited
Unit 8 Amherst Business Centre
Budbrooke Road
Warwick
CV34 5WE
England
Tel. 01926 499 619
Email: info@helion.co.uk
Website: www.helion.co.uk
Twitter: @helionbooks
Visit our blog http://blog.helion.co.uk/

Text © Vladimir Kotelnikov 2024
Photographs © see note on page 48
Colour profiles © Andrey Yurgenson 2024
Maps drawn by George Anderson © Helion
     & Company 2024

Designed and typeset by Farr out
     Publications, Wokingham, Berkshire
Cover design by Paul Hewitt, Battlefield
     Design (www.battlefield-design.co.uk)

Every reasonable effort has been made to
trace copyright holders and to obtain their
permission for the use of copyright material.
The author and publisher apologise for any
errors or omissions in this work, and would
be grateful if notified of any corrections that
should be incorporated in future reprints or
editions of this book.

ISBN 978-1-804516-08-9

British Library Cataloguing-in-Publication
     Data
A catalogue record for this book is available
     from the British Library

We always welcome receiving book
proposals from prospective authors.

CONTENTS

T0408294

Note: In order to simplify the use of this book, all names, locations and geographic
designations are as provided in *The Times World Atlas*, or other traditionally accepted
major sources of reference, as of the time of described events.

ABBREVIATIONS

CAMD   Central Asian Military District
NKVD   People's Commissariat for Internal Affairs (*Narodny Komissariat Vnutrennikh Del*)
OGPU   Joint State Political Directorate (*Obyedinyonnoye Gosudarstvennoye Politicheskoye Upravleniye*)

RSFSR   Russian Soviet Federative Socialist Republic (*Rossiyskaya Sovetskaya Federativnaya Socialisticheskaya Respublika*)

INTRODUCTION

While other great powers were in search of colonies across the oceans, Russia was gradually expanding its territorial borders. Starting from the middle of the nineteenth century the country began annexing territories in Central Asia, its northern part had already been controlled by the Russians.

The Kyrgyz were nomadic herdsmen who did not build cities or use a written language of their own. Their social system was based on clan-tribal relations rather than the feudal system; moreover, the Kyrgyz did not have a unified state and for them transition to Russian rule meant recognition of the supremacy of the Russian Tsar by the tribal chiefs who agreed to pay tribute to the Russian state. This process was proceeding quite peacefully. The first three *zhuzes* (clans) of the Kyrgyz had sworn an oath to the Empress Anna Ioanovna as early as 1738.

The Kazakhs were at a similar stage of social development. The word 'Kazakh' did not even exist then; the people were called Kyrgyz-Kaisaks and rarely mentioned as a separate ethnic group. In official documents both the Kyrgyz and the Kazakhs were referred to as 'Siberian Kyrgyz' people. In 1822 the *Charter on the Siberian Kyrgyz people* was adopted: it subordinated their tribes to the administration of the Omsk Oblast of the West-Siberian Governorate General. In the 1850s many Kazakhs and Kyrgyz started taking Russian citizenship.

Southward there were three major states – the Kokand and the Khiva khanates and the Emirate of Bukhara. Though all three states were multi-ethnic, the Uzbeks (then called Sarts by the Russians) prevailed among their population. The states had a feudal way of life and also practiced slavery. The Kokand Khanate occupied parts of the present-day Uzbekistan, Tajikistan, Kyrgyzstan, Kazakhstan, and even Chinese Xinjiang. The expansion of Russia to the south and spreading of its authority to the tribes that had previously paid tribute to the Khan of Kokand triggered non-stop border conflicts. The Kokands raided the encampments of the 'renegade' tribes, pillaged the caravans of Russian merchants that travelled to and from China under the protection of armed guards, and even raided deep into Russian territory, attacking the settlements and selling captured people into slavery.

In an attempt to defend the border, Russia built a chain of small fortresses; however, it was only a passive solution to the problem. Eventually the issue was resolved in a radical way by sending troops against Kokand. On 17 May 1865 a Russian army seized Tashkent and the Khan had to cede it, together with the adjoining territory, to Russia. In 1868 a Russian-Kokand trade treaty was concluded thus greatly improving the situation for Russian merchants.

In 1875 a *coup d'état* occurred in Kokand bringing to power the aggressive Nasruddin Khan. He demanded that Russia renegotiate the treaties and return to the previous borders. Not limiting himself to those demands, he sent his troops to the routes between Tashkent and Khojent, where Nasruddin's warriors robbed and killed travellers, enslaved them and burned post stations along the road. The response was fast. The Russian army went on the offensive, defeating the backward Kokand forces by the end of September 1875. The military action resulted in the seizure of new lands from Kokand. In January 1876 Tsar Alexander II ordered complete abolition of the Khanate, transforming it into the Fergana Province under the administration of the Governor-General.

The other two state entities in Central Asia were also in conflict with Russia, but partly retained their independence. The Khanate of Khiva (also known as Khorezm), like Kokand, was a constant source of trouble to the Russian authorities. The first military campaign against Khiva was organised by Tsar Peter I as early as 1717; the outcome was extremely unsuccessful. In the spring of 1873, General K.N. Kaufman sent four groups of troops from Tashkent, Orenburg, Mangyshlak, and Krasnovodsk against the Khan of Khiva. On 29 May Khiva was seized. Under the peace treaty part of the Khanate was separated and received the status of a Russian protectorate in August. The Russian authorities demanded abolition of slavery and immediately liberated and evacuated all slaves who were Russian citizens.

The Emirate of Bukhara occupied parts of the present-day Uzbekistan, Tajikistan and Turkmenistan. In March 1868, Emir Muafar declared *ghazavat* (holy religious war) on the Russians, though this cost him dearly, and as early as May the Emir's army was defeated. On 22 June he declared himself a vassal of the Russian Empire. In September 1873, Bukhara was granted a protectorate status.

Fortified garrisons appeared in the occupied territories followed by the construction of railways and telegraph lines. Modern hospitals, pharmacies and schools appeared, serving primarily for the needs of Russian settlers. Officials, policemen, doctors and engineers were sent from Russia to serve in Central Asia and Russian settlements were established, with peasants lured there by the allocation of land and various benefits. In addition, Central Asia became a place for both criminal and political exiles. The term 'Russians' in this case refers to all peoples of the multinational empire, and in particular, many of the exiles came from Ukraine; they built their villages retaining unique national architectural styles. The settlers mostly tried to stay near military garrisons and important roads.

New enclaves populated by newcomers from Russia appeared in the cities. They were usually built close to the old town according to the customary Russian standards – more spacious, greener, more orderly. As a rule, military barracks were located close to each other,

Locals obsequiously greet the Russian Governor-General and his attendants.

if possible, on the dominant heights. This allowed the artillery to easily bombard the old town if the need arose.

In the Fergana region the old judicial and administrative system was retained for a long time; in Khiva and Bukhara the social system was not altered at all. The local tribes were allowed to have their own small armies. The Russian authorities only tried to eradicate the most savage vestiges of local customs, such as the stoning of unfaithful wives. In Tashkent, one woman was punished for being unfaithful to her husband by being thrown in a sack from the roof of the tallest building in the city: the Madrasah (an Islamic religious school). As a penance, the Governor-General ordered the top two floors of the building to be demolished.

Relations between the locals and the newcomers were far from unclouded. First, land for settlers was confiscated from the native population on various pretexts. The Tsarist decrees of 1886 and 1891 made most of the land public. A family of 'natives' was allocated 15 dessiatina's (a land measure equivalent to 2.7 acres) of land as an indefinite tenancy. Some poor people benefited from this, the wealthier people, on the contrary, lost. Secondly, the way of life of the newcomers was in many ways inconsistent with the requirements of the highly influential Muslim religion in Central Asia. In particular, Russian women dressed differently, behaved differently and could even hold some positions in education and health care. Russians drank alcohol and bred pigs which are, according to the Koran, unclean animals. The Ukrainians were particularly active in pig-breeding and could not imagine a borsch without a piece of lard. Thirdly, the locals were reluctant to embrace the efforts of the Russian authorities to improve sanitary conditions. Almost entirely illiterate,

they defended their customary norms of life and feared doctors and nurses. They were also negative about secular education, which until then had been purely religious.

Most of the population (95 percent) was engaged in agriculture, with herders comprising a quarter of the whole number. Less than 5 percent were literate. There was no written native language, and the mullahs (local Islamic priests) read and wrote in Arabic.

The number of people coming from Russia grew rapidly, reaching 200,000 in 1897 and quadrupling 10 years later. Taking advantage of the privileges granted by the authorities, many of the first-wave migrants turned into wealthy peasants (kulaks) who exploited the labour of the local poor.

Conflicts increased after the outbreak of the First World War. The army requisitioned the livestock, paying no more than 10 percent of the market value. But the real explosion was triggered by the decree of Tsar Nikolai II 'On requisition of non-Russian population' which was issued on 25 June 1916. It required conscription of the indigenous population – who were not subject to military service – for working in the rear. Uzbeks, Tajiks, Kazakhs and others did not want to go anywhere to help in somebody else's war. In addition, the principle of compiling the lists was irritating – they tried to include poor people who did not have their own families.

The first riot took place on 4 July 1916 in Khojent, where a mob of Tajiks attacked representatives of the authorities and then all Russians. The uprising soon spread to almost all of Central Asia. Rebel gangs raided and burned villages of settlers, brutally killing the elderly, women and children, destroyed railway stations and tore up telegraph lines. Traffic on the roads was paralysed and any

Russian national could become a victim. Mullahs called on Muslims for *ghazavat* against 'infidels'. The rebels therefore ravaged Christian churches and monasteries murdering their priests and monks.

According to some authors, agents of German and Turkish intelligence contributed to fomenting the fighting. Chinese revolutionaries transported some 300 activists from Xinjiang and delivered weapons and ammunition. Martial law was declared in the Turkestan Military District. Troops with machine guns and artillery were deployed to suppress the rebellion. They fairly quickly defeated the main forces of the rebels as the latter were poorly organised and armed. The prisoners were tried by military tribunals, but lynching by the Russian settlers was also not uncommon. Fearing reprisals, some 300,000 people crossed the border into China. The uprising prompted a new massive requisitioning of land. Sporadic skirmishes with small rebel groups continued until February 1917.

1
TWO REVOLUTIONS AND A CIVIL WAR

The February 1917 bourgeois revolution, which led to the abdication of Tsar Nicholai II, revived the moods towards independence for the Central Asian states. The Emirate of Bukhara declared secession; this move was approved by the Russian Provisional Government.

Even more confusion and unrest were caused by the Bolshevik October Revolution. Tashkent was the centre of the revolutionary movement in Central Asia where the Bolsheviks and leftist Social Revolutionaries organised a council. The supporters of the old government (they became known as the Whites) sent a punitive expedition to the city: a group of mostly Cossacks led by General Korovichenko. They managed to disarm one of the two regiments stationed in the town and attacked the so-called 'Freedom House' where the council was holding a meeting. Soldiers of the 1st Siberian Regiment and volunteers, who joined the Red Guard, were able to repulse them. Four days of battles culminated in the surrender of the last White stronghold, the old fortress. Then the Reds seized power in Krasnovodsk, Chardzhou and New Bukhara (Kagan). In December they seized Samarkand, Ashgabat and Skobelev (Fergana).

But the Whites were unwilling to surrender and engaged regiments of Semirechensk and Orenburg Cossacks drawn from Iran. In January 1918 the Cossacks took Chardzhui and Samarkand and approached Tashkent. However, the Reds managed to defeat them. In April 1918 the Turkestan Soviet Autonomous Republic (within Russia) was proclaimed. It was divided into Transcaspian, Samarkand, Semirechensk, Syr-Darya and Fergana regions.

In the spring of 1918, a coup d'état took place in the Khanate of Khiva, organised by Junaid Khan, a Turkmen of the Yomud tribe. The history of this man is quite remarkable, and he will appear in this story again. As early as 1912 Junaid Khan formed his first gang and robbed caravans in the desert. The scale of his activity expanded and gradually, by the end of 1917, his gang of over 1,500 people resembled a small army. Junaid Khan had acquired a certain status in Khiva, and at the same time made many enemies during his struggle for power. Having entered the service of Khiva Khan, he became a *serdar-karim*, a commander of the local army. However, this was not enough for Junaid Khan; in March 1918 he assassinated Asfandiyar Khan and enthroned his uncle Sayyid Abdullah. The latter however was only a nominal ruler and it was Junaid Khan who was the real decision-maker.

The moment seemed convenient to regain the lands on the right bank of the Amu-Darya, previously ceded to Russia. On 20 September the Khan's troops seized and ravaged Novo-Urgench; in November they besieged Petro-Alexandrovsk (present-day Turtkul). They were resisted by units of the Red Guard and several major defeats forced Junaid Khan to sit down at the negotiating table.

Junaid Khan, *de facto* ruler of Bukhara.

Here, the first appearance of aircraft was recorded. One Sopwith 1½-Strutter was delivered by barge along the Amu-Darya to Petro-Alexandrovsk. From there the airplane was to fly to Khiva (about 80km away). V.S. Vakhmistrov, who later became a famous aircraft designer and creator of the *Zveno* 'flying aircraft carrier', was the observer on board this aircraft. The crew took off safely, but halfway through the flight they hit a blizzard and got lost and the airplane circled for about an hour until the pilot regained his bearings before the 1½-Strutter reached Khiva. The next day the pilots found out that for a while they had been flying near the village where the negotiations with representatives of Junaid Khan were being held. Frightened by the plane, the enemy had made major concessions. According to the agreement signed, they were to abandon the captured lands and release the prisoners; however, the looted goods were never returned by the people of Khiva.

In Bukhara in March 1918 the Reds organised an uprising, but the Emir's troops suppressed it. The Emirate concluded a treaty with the Turkestan Republic confirming Bukhara's independence. In mid-1918 the Civil War that was already raging in Russia reached Central Asia. Units of the Red Army organised by the Bolsheviks confronted the troops of various White governments that had emerged on the outskirts of the country and the British interventionists who had taken up positions on the Caspian Sea. It was during the Civil War that aviation began to be used in Central Asia.

The Reds had the 15th Air Unit, which operated four Farman 30 reconnaissance aircraft with Salmson engines and two Nieuport 21 fighters. The unit was commanded by N.N. Starodumov. The Farman 30 was a biplane with the tail of truss structure. The crew of two and the engine were accommodated in a nacelle mounted between the upper and lower wings. A water-cooled Salmson engine (150–160hp) drove the propeller. A pilot sat in the nacelle at the front, with an observer behind him. The latter had a machine gun, which was used for firing from a standing position. Those aircraft were built under French licence by the Dux Factory in Moscow. The Farman 30 (also known as 'Fartry') was from the end of 1916 the main type of reconnaissance aircraft in the Russian aviation. The aircraft did not excel in high speed or manoeuvrability but was considered reliable and had a good flying range and a decent payload. Nieuport 21s were imported from France during the First World War. It was a typical biplane fighter of the time with Le Rhone 9C rotary engine (80hp), armed with a single machine gun. Pilots loved this machine for its good handling and flying characteristics.

However the airplanes and especially their engines were badly worn, and there was a shortage of spare parts. Paskutskiy, the chairman of the Revolutionary Military Council of the Transcaspian Front later wrote: 'The airplanes... that we inherited from the former Tsarist aviation had already been battered during the imperialist war and long past their service life; they were literally "flying coffins"...'

In the course of the Civil War Central Asia was gradually surrounded by a ring of fronts. The Transcaspian Front was the first to emerge in the west of the Turkestan Republic. There, from the summer of 1918, the Reds were battling with the Whites and British units of General Malleson and Brigadier General Beatty who disembarked on the eastern shore of the Caspian Sea and forced the Reds to retreat to Merv.

In July 1918 one Farman with pilot N.N. Starodumov and observer M. Leonov was flown to a site on the right bank of the Amu-Darya, between Chardzhou (present-day Türkmenabat) and Farad stations. From there they carried out reconnaissance missions which involved photography. By this time the Reds had launched an offensive and the airfields were changing as the troops advanced. It is interesting that Starodumov was the Chief of Aviation of Turkestan Republic since 17 May 1918 but he kept flying on missions in person.

There were no bombs in the unit's stocks and it was impossible to obtain them from Russia at the time. Machine-gun technician T. Kharitonov proposed to convert three-inch and six-inch artillery shells into bombs by attaching homemade stabilisers to them. Those bombs would go deep in the ground when dropped and proved ineffective, but there were no other options.

While retreating, the Whites dismantled the railway tracks and carried away the rails and sleepers. On 10 August Starodumov was given the mission of preventing that. Not far from Bairam-Ali station he discovered the trains that were loaded with the rails and other railroad equipment. The pilot decided to destroy the railway track behind the trains and paralyse the railway traffic. There were three high-explosive 16kg bombs on board and the observer, Leonov, dropped them 'by eye' with his hands, without any aiming device. They made three approaches, dropped three bombs and missed the rails. The trains started moving westward, while the plane pursued them, firing a machine gun. And then a miracle happened: the lead train crashed into a train already standing at the station. Either the driver was killed or the braking system was damaged. Two more trains, one after another, crashed into the mess. The old Farman returned to the base with a dozen bullet holes.

On 18 August 1918 one Nieuport 21 fighter, flown by pilot I. Chernyy, joined the hostilities. From a site near Tejen station the aviators conducted reconnaissance flights and fired machine guns at the enemy and sometimes they dropped hand grenades. The aircraft broke down several times but were repaired again. The fighting was unevenly successful – the Whites and British again went on the offensive and in early November gradually approached Chardzhou. The Reds took up defence there, and the front remained static for a long time.

At the end of March 1919, the 43rd Air Unit – that had a similar composition to the battered 15th – made its way to Turkestan, so the two detachments were merged into one. On 14 May 1919, the Red Army attacked the enemy and advanced westward. The Transcaspian Front units were supported by only one serviceable aircraft, a Farman 30 with pilot N.S. Gorbunov and observer V.R. Braunets, which was based at a temporary airfield near Uch-Adzhi station. From there they conducted reconnaissance flights; at first the observer simply sketched enemy positions, and later photography was used. In one case, a Farman was involved in adjustment of artillery fire. A radio station was installed on the aircraft and a female radio operator was taken on board. Her name was Bystrova and this was not typical of the then military aviation. The aircraft was used to adjust artillery fire in the battle at Annenkovo station and performed combat operations up to the approach of the Red Army units to Merv, where Braunets sketched the outlines of fortifications. On 23 May the engine failed in flight and the aircraft crashed during a forced landing.

In June several more airplanes of the 43rd Unit joined the flights on the Transcaspian Front. The Reds were advancing along the only existing railway line, and the pace of the advance either accelerated or slowed down depending on the condition of the railway track bed. A significant halt was caused by the destruction of the railway between Bami and Geok-Tepe by the Whites and it was not until mid-September that it was restored and the troops moved on.

On 12 November the crew of the pilot Starodumov received the order to attack an enemy armoured train. He spotted it at Uzun-Su station (according to another document – at Iskander station) together with a small train composed of four passenger cars, which he identified as a mobile headquarters. The station was defended by anti-aircraft artillery which opened fire on the airplane. Two bombs were dropped, one hit the staff carriage, killing three officers and wounding four others. The Farman sustained some damage from bursting anti-aircraft shells, while on the way back it was fired upon three times by the White's Nieuport, which added several more bullet holes.

As of 1 December, only two aircraft remained in service in the Red unit, but on 6 December a Nieuport 21 fighter was captured at Kazanjik Station.

At the end of 1918 yet another front, the Aktyubinsk Front, emerged, as Admiral A.V. Kolchak's army was advancing westwards from Siberia. As early as the beginning of 1919 communication between Eastern Turkestan and the rest of Soviet Russia became difficult as White Cossacks were moving in the steppes, intercepting messengers. Thus, the Reds decided to use aircraft. On 9 January 1919, near Martuk station (near Aktyubinsk) a Farman 30 biplane, which had been assembled from two damaged examples, took off. On board were the pilot N.S. Gorbunov and the observer V.R. Braunets, who were carrying letters for the Eastern Front Headquarters. They had no map, only a handwritten pencil sketch and the aircraft simply followed the tracks of the Turkestan railway. Trying to avoid encountering enemy airplanes near Orenburg, the pilot decided to bypass the city. As a result, he lost his bearings but managed to

Pilot N.S. Gorbunov in the front cockpit of a Farman 30 biplane, Chief of Staff of the Transcaspian Front I.V. Yefimov in the rear cockpit, June 1919.

and continued his way forward. The next morning he was found on the railway tracks near the Reds' location. By the evening of the second day a search and rescue party found Gorbunov with frostbitten legs and they had to be amputated.

By that time the airplanes and engines were worn out and the Transcaspian Front commanders asked for replenishment – one reconnaissance aircraft and one fighter.

One of the air units which became available after the defeat of Kolchak, the 11th Air Squadron under the command of V.S. Rutkovskiy, arrived in Turkestan. The unit operated Sopwith 1½-Strutters and captured German LVG reconnaissance airplanes. Sopwith aircraft had a good reputation for reliability, speed, significant operational range and bomb load. In mid-January 1920 a combined unit of three aircraft – LVG, Farman 30 and Sopwith – was deployed at Jebel station. Then part of the 25th Air Unit was relocated there as well, and on 8 February another LVG arrived. From 20 January those forces conducted reconnaissance flights, carried out bombing missions and machine-gunned the enemy troops. The British were no longer in Krasnovodsk – in April 1919 Britain started withdrawing its troops to Iran and the last British soldiers left Krasnovodsk in August.

find the way back to the railway after Orenburg and determined the aircraft position by flying low and reading the station names. Then low cloud cover again forced the pilot to fly below 100m. At the end, Gorbunov landed at Novosergeevka station, in the rear of the Reds. The flight had taken four hours with about 300km of flying over the enemy-controlled territory. The crew members were awarded Orders of the Red Banner and received monetary rewards.

In mid-April 1919 Kolchak's army completely cut off Central Asia from the European part of Russia. The Reds continued to use aviation to link Central Asia with Central Russia. One day in May 1919 pilot I.A. Buob (according to another document 'Buoba') was delivering documents to the station Chelkar in Turkestan. He arrived there safely, but on his way back got into a storm, used up all fuel and made a forced landing near Iletsk, 100–120km away from the destination, where the White garrison was located. The pilots were taken prisoner. The passenger who was a political officer was immediately executed, and Buob was sentenced to death too but was kept in prison for some time. When the Red Army launched an offensive, the enemy started executing the prisoners, but Buob managed to escape; he hid in the steppes until his comrades arrived. He was later awarded the Order of the Red Banner.

In the summer of 1919 Kolchak's army started retreating. In mid-September the Aktyubinsk Front merged with the Turkestan Front of the Red Army (a new name of the Southern Group of the Eastern Front) and Central Asia's links with Russia began to be restored.

In January 1920 Red troops approached Krasnovodsk, and their aircraft bombed the town. On 2 January, the crew of N.S. Gorbunov and I.V. Efimov raided the enemy troops on the outskirts of Krasnovodsk. The return fire caused some damage to the plane – one bullet went through the radiator and the water drained out, causing the overheated engine to jam. The pilot flew away from the railway to avoid enemy soldiers and made a forced landing on the sand dunes near the Iranian border. The aircraft was wrecked, but the crew suffered only bruises. They damaged the airplane further, removed the machine gun and the camera, and buried them in the sand. Then the crew went eastward. Once they ran into an enemy patrol and hid in the sand. Due to exhaustion Gorbunov refused to go further, so Efimov gave his comrade his felt boots and a fur jacket

reconnaissance airplanes. Sopwith aircraft had a good reputation for reliability, speed, significant operational range and bomb load. In mid-January 1920 a combined unit of three aircraft – LVG, Farman 30 and Sopwith – was deployed at Jebel station. Then part of the 25th Air Unit was relocated there as well, and on 8 February another LVG arrived. From 20 January those forces conducted reconnaissance flights, carried out bombing missions and machine-gunned the enemy troops. The British were no longer in Krasnovodsk – in April 1919 Britain started withdrawing its troops to Iran and the last British soldiers left Krasnovodsk in August.

Prior to the bombing raids on the city, pilot A.D. Chernakov on the Farman 30 conducted a reconnaissance flight over Krasnovodsk with Chief of Staff of the Transcaspian Front I.V. Yefimov on board and they inspected and photographed the enemy defence fortifications and positions. During the following days the aircraft carried out reconnaissance combined with bombing, usually with two or three 16kg bombs taken on board. In addition to the bombs, leaflets were dropped calling for surrender. On the morning of 6 February, two Sopwith airplanes (piloted by N.P. Ilzin and I.I. Chernyy) of the 25th Air Unit carried out air strike on the approaches to Krasnovodsk. They dropped bombs on the Whites and fired on them with machine guns. Then the soldiers of the Red Army went on the attack.

After a landing site near Krasnovodsk station was seized, all airplanes of the Red Army were deployed there. From this airfield they attacked the ships that were anchored offshore and which were bombarding the Reds. When attacked from the air, the ships usually moved away from the shore. On 15 February, despite heavy anti-aircraft fire, a direct hit on an armed steamer was achieved, and the ship was covered with a cloud of smoke and steam.

By the end of the month, the Transcaspian region was completely cleared of the Whites. However, the aviation continued to patrol over the sea in search of enemy ships. For example, in April they spotted the steamer *Australia*; its crew mutinied and later brought the ship to Krasnovodsk. Such flights were considered rather dangerous as the land-based aircraft flew 100–150km away from the shore. Given the low reliability of aviation equipment at the time, especially engines, those concerns were quite reasonable.

In May, the Red Army achieved a series of victories in the south, and on 24 May 1920 seized Kushka at the border with Afghanistan. The Transcaspian Front ceased to exist.

In the meantime, Junaid Khan was trying to reinforce his troops. He received military aid from Kolchak in the form of 1,500 rifles, nine machine guns and one cannon. In November 1919 an uprising shook Khiva and the Red Army, which had released some forces from the closed fronts, supported the rebels. As a result, Junaid

Khan's forces were defeated. On 2 February 1920 Said Abdullah Khan formally abdicated the throne. On 26 April the Khorezm People's Soviet Republic was proclaimed; while retaining its autonomy, it was, however, part of the Russian Soviet Federative Socialist Republic (RSFSR). Junaid Khan, with the remnants of his troops, fled to the Kara-Kum Desert. Then more than once, like a phoenix, he would regain his forces again and try to reverse the situation. He was defeated, fled and then returned several times over.

2

BASMACHI

In February and March 1919, near Kokand the Reds for the first time encountered local insurgent units, which became known as *Basmachi* (translated as 'raiders'). In the 1920s they were sometimes incorrectly referred to as *Bakhmachi*. The slogans and later the actual policy of the Soviet authorities irritated many local residents. The wealthy were not happy with the land (and water) reform and the inclusion of representatives of the poor in the administrative authorities. The clergy opposed the separation of church from the state. The conservatives were infuriated by the declaration of women's equality; the Bolsheviks abolished the *paranja* (the Central Asia equivalent to the burqa) and allowed girls to go to school together with boys. The growing fight against illiteracy made previously uneducated and oppressed people more socially-conscious, committed to fight for their rights.

The number of unhappy people increased due to numerous mistakes and failures of the authorities: there were very few more or less educated local residents, and the emissaries dispatched from Russia neither spoke the languages nor knew the customs. This triggered constant conflicts. There was even a group of local nationals among the Turkestan Bolsheviks demanding not only the removal of Russian leaders but also the withdrawal from Turkestan of all military units not manned by Muslims.

Ordinary bandits were also considered to be *Basmachi*, and there were plenty of those on the outskirts of the vast country. Their ultimate dream was to raid a caravan of goods or rob a shop in a village where they could steal a box of soap and a few boxes of cheap chocolates. Such bandits would sometimes attack policemen or military personnel in order to seize weapons and ammunition.

The *Basmachi* were initially concentrated around Fergana. Gangs of 500–600 men were considered large; usually only two-thirds of them (*dzhigits*) had firearms. The rest were called 'stick-men' because they were armed only with strong sticks and knives. Even the *dzhigits* did not often carry Russian magazine-fed three-line rifles (the Mosin-Nagant rifle). Old Berdan single-shot rifles and equally outdated French Gras rifles prevailed. Quite a few fighters used *moultuks* – handmade rifles. Only a few gangs connected with British intelligence had a significant number of modern weapons but machine guns were a rarity even among them, and the *Basmachi* had no artillery at all. Interestingly, sabres were even rarer than firearms. The commanders of the *Basmachi* were usually members of the local nobility, the *begs* (*beks* or *beys*, a Turkish title). Some of them had advisers from the former White officers. Large gangs consisted of units headed by *kurbashis*. There was no clear structure – a *kurbashi* could command five or a hundred *dzhigits*. Most of the gangs consisted of ten to 50 men; Madamin Bek and Irgash (Ergash) led the largest gangs.

The abundance of horses gave the *Basmachi* a high degree of mobility. They also had the advantage of excellent knowledge of the terrain and maintained multiple tribal ties with the local population. The gangs raided settlements, killed Soviet officials, communists, policemen and local activists, and looted everything they could find. The commanders of some larger gangs established ties with the British intelligence. Money, weapons and ammunition were delivered to them through Bukhara.

In April 1919 the *Basmachi* approached Namangan and, after an assault action, seized the old town. However, they were repulsed by hastily deployed Red Army units.

The Soviet leaders tried to put out the fire. The *Basmachi* were promised amnesty if they laid down their arms and went home. But that plan failed – in the summer of 1919 Madamin Bek united many of the gangs into the Muslim People's Army.

Since the actions of *Basmachi* were mainly directed against relocated Russian nationals, self-defence units appeared in the Fergana Valley. In November 1918 they united into the Peasant Army, headed by K. I. Monstrov, with headquarters situated in Jalalabad. The government of the Turkestan Republic allocated equipment, weapons and ammunition for these troops. Later, those who served in the Peasant Army were paid as Red Army servicemen. Interestingly, there were no commissars or political officers in that army as Monstrov stubbornly adhered to the principle of non-partisanship. The Peasant Army was subordinated to the command of the Fergana Front organised against the *Basmachi*, headed by M.V. Safonov. At first the self-defence units provided substantial assistance to the Red Army.

However, the Russian settlers had a generally negative attitude towards the Soviet authorities. They did not like the fact that they abolished their privileges and even granted some advantages to local national groups. The economic policy of the Bolsheviks multiplied the number of opposition members. The state monopoly of bread imposed by Bolsheviks on 25 June 1919 was in fact a robbery of peasants. Ration squads raided the villages confiscating 'surplus food', i.e. everything above the minimum survival stocks to last until the next harvest. In some places those actions caused famine.

The Turkestan authorities made two attempts to disarm the units of the Peasant Army but failed. At the same time, the cautious and calculating Madamin Bek began to look for reconciliation with Monstrov. He forbade his units to attack the settlers and even attacked the Khal Khoji *Basmachi*, who were massacring the Russians. His efforts paid off. Monstrov broke with the Reds and on 1 September 1919 concluded a treaty with Madamin Bek to unite the forces; they had a total of about 20,000 fighters at that time. The

Madamin Bek, the son of the last Kokand khan, in his younger years.

A small group of Turkmen *Basmachi*.

allies established contacts with representatives of Admiral Kolchak who promised military assistance.

The united armies quickly seized Osh, with the Red garrison partly siding with the enemy and partly surrendering without resistance. Safonov, commander of the Fergana Front, personally led his forces towards Osh, but was defeated in a counter-attack in the Aravan Gorge and retreated with great difficulty. Madamin Bek and Monstrov launched an offensive against Andijan, Skobelev (Fergana) and Namangan. They succeeded in taking almost all of Andijan, but on 22 September the Kazan Combined Regiment came to the aid of the besieged. When the Reds took to the offensive, the men of Monstrov's army began to flee to their homes; Osh was surrendered without a fight. On 30 September the Red Army seized Jalalabad. The former allies quarrelled, the *Basmachi* of Madamin Bek attacked the remnants of the Peasant Army. Having no more troops, Monstrov surrendered to the Reds in January 1921.

Madamin Bek, who had about 7,000 men, settled near the border fortress of Gulcha, where he obtained assistance from the British, providing money, arms and ammunition. Having recovered from defeats, his army resumed their raids. They burned cotton mills and people's houses, destroyed railway tracks and stole cattle.

Gradually, the closure of other fronts allowed the Reds to draw in large military forces. The Fergana Front was liquidated and the coordination of operations was carried out by M.V. Frunze, commander of the Turkestan Front, who was replaced by G.Y. Sokolnikov in September 1920. The 2nd Turkestan Division became the main striking force. Garrisons were deployed in large settlements; roads and adjacent areas were patrolled by mobile detachments and 'flying squads', while self-defence squads were formed of local volunteers. At first they were hesitant to give firearms to the Central Asians who were therefore called 'Red stick-men'. Later, rifles were entrusted to some of the local nationals and the self-defence groups were given the more honourable name of *kyzyl-askers*, i.e. 'Red soldiers'.

In May 1920, the 26th Air Unit under the command of A. Stepanov was relocated to Turkestan. In July two of its battered Sopwith aircraft began to provide air support to the troops of the Samarkand-Bukhara group. The airplanes flew to the border town of Termez. They would take-off directly from the central square of the city, around which the treetops had to be cut down. One flight was particularly successful when Stepanov spotted a column of the *Basmachi* on the road by the bank of the Vakhsh River; it consisted of up to 1,000 horses (including pack-horses). Observer E. Ukhin dropped bombs on it and fired a machine gun. Soon, three planes repeated the raid – they dropped about twenty 20lb bombs on the *Basmachi*, who were moving along the gorge, and fired on them. Stepanov later wrote: 'Splinters of bombs and rocks plunged into the bandits. The horses, frightened by the explosions and roaring engines, rushed away from the village, trampling the *Basmachi* who were trying to catch them'. At the signal from the plane, a red rocket, the Red cavalrymen who had been in ambush went in to attack. The gang suffered significant losses, some 300 men were killed and about 100 drowned trying to swim across the Vakhsh.

Near Kabedian, pilot Chuchin attacked a caravan of weapons moving from Afghanistan. He managed to disperse the enemy with machine-gun fire, but the plane was hit by rifle fire in return. Two bullets pierced the cabin floor between the pilot's legs.

It should be noted that the pilots had to fly on extremely worn-out aircraft. Aircraft technician A.A. Tokarev later wrote: 'Our "Sopwith" airplane ... was old, time-worn, and had up to seventy patches of all kinds, as well as mice-eaten main wing spars and control pedals'.

In September 1920 Junaid Khan gathered a new gang and re-joined the game, so troops had to be sent against him as well. The hostilities went with varying success, but overall, the activity of the enemy gradually decreased. On 31 January 1921 Makhkan Khodja's and Akber Ali's gangs surrendered, a total of about 600 armed men and 2,000 'stick-men'. At the beginning of March Madamin Bek also surrendered. He was amnestied, but then fell into the hands of his enemy, Khal Khoji, and was beheaded. About 2,000 *Basmachi* remained active, scattered in inaccessible areas. In particular, Junaid Khan continued to raid small settlements.

At the same time the authorities changed their policy towards the population. *Prodrazverstka* (confiscation of grain and other agricultural products from peasants at nominal fixed prices according to specified quotas by the Soviet state during the Civil

War period of 1918–1921) was abolished, replaced by in-kind (agricultural products) taxation of the peasants. Some taxes were abolished altogether. Grain was brought to the areas where it was in short supply. In January 1920 the chairman of *Sovnarkom* (Council of People's Commissars) Lenin sent a letter to Turkestan in which he wrote: 'Instead of commanding, we should show in practice that the workers of Russia renounce the policy pursued by tsarism, and it has

to be done with the greatest tolerance and trust to the local people'. Later he also wrote: 'It is critically important to win the trust of the natives, three times and four times to gain...'.

All those efforts led to a dramatic decline in the activity of the *Basmachi*. For example, in November 1920 not a single attack on the railways was recorded, whereas in September there had been 17 raids.

3
THE END OF THE EMIRATE OF BUKHARA

After separation from Russia, the Emir of Bukhara started pursuing an openly hostile policy. It was through Bukhara that British intelligence delivered weapons, ammunition and money to the *Basmachi*. The internal situation in the Emirate was unstable, as the revolutionary events in the adjacent areas encouraged people to strive for reforms and look for new ways. The Russian settlements of Novaya Bukhara (Kagan), Novyi Chardjui, and Termez (Kerki), controlled by the Reds, were situated on the territory of the Emirate. In March 1918 there was an uprising in Bukhara which the authorities suppressed successfully. This was followed by a treaty

signed with the Turkestan government recognising the Emirate's independence.

The Bukhara army was trained by Turkish and British military advisers, with weapons supplied from abroad. Thus, in January 1920 the British delivered from Mashhad 1,200 rifles, 12 machine guns, four cannons as well as ammunition and shells. The British were pushing the Emir into action against Turkestan, promising additional military assistance. M.V. Frunze reported to Moscow in early August 1920: 'Bukhara... is now becoming clearly hostile to us and is openly shaking weapons'.

In May 1920, pilot Shpak of the 43rd Air Unit, stationed at Kagan, went missing. His plane was found by the railway tracks, but the pilot was not there. It turned out that he had been lured into a village and stabbed to death.

On 22 August the aviation of the Turkestan Front conducted a demonstration of power over Old Bukhara. During the parade of the Emir's troops, four aircraft of the 43rd Air Unit flew over the city. They took photographs of the parading troops and scattered leaflets. The Emir issued an ultimatum, demanding the withdrawal of Red Army units from Kagan, Karshi and from the exclusion zone of the Central Asian railway.

On 28 August 1920 a new uprising began in Bukhara. The rebels had some 7,000 armed men, the Emir could deploy 16,000 soldiers and 27,000 fighters from the irregular units of his vassal *beks*. Moscow considered it a convenient occasion to solve the problem for good. Frunze ordered an offensive – his forces included 9,500 men, five armoured trains, several armoured cars, 40 guns and 11 airplanes. Those 11 aircraft represented the entire serviceable fleet of the 25th, 26th and 43rd Air Units. At that time, the 43rd Air Unit was stationed in New Bukhara (Kagan), the 25th in Chardzhou and the 26th in Samarkand. All aircraft were ordered to be relocated

Aerial photo of Bukhara, 1920.

Head of Air Force of Turkestan Front, V.Yu. Yungmeister.

Bukhara *sarbaz* (soldiers of the Emir's regular army) and their officer, 1920.

The aircraft of the 25th Air Unit are being prepared for a bombing raid on Bukhara, Kagan airfield, August 1920

Field headquarters at Kagan airfield; commander of the 43rd Air Unit, I.I. Chernyy on the far right. Late August 1920.

with one bomb. The *sarbazes* (Bukhara's soldiers) fired their rifles intensively into the air damaging some aircraft. One Sopwith airplane was out of operation though it was not the enemy's fault – a torn off rod deformed the engine cowl. Pilot Stolyarov did not return from one of his missions on a Nieuport 17 fighter, which had been assembled from the airplanes at Kagan airfield decommissioned due to wear and tear. Three hours later the pilot returned – on a donkey – as a stalled engine forced him to make an emergency landing.

On 2 September the rebels and Red Army soldiers seized the fortress at Old Bukhara. The Emir and his personal guard (about 1,000 horsemen) marched eastwards into the Pamir Mountains. Pilots dropped several bombs on a column of cavalry and a large convoy.

During the fighting for Bukhara the Red aviation made 59 flights and dropped 170 bombs, but by the end of the campaign only three or four serviceable airplanes remained. Two Farmans were crashed, the Voisin's engine was unserviceable. Yungmeister and five pilots and observers were awarded the Order of the Red Banner, while many others received gold watches and other valuable gifts.

After the overthrow of the Emir, the Bukhara People's Soviet Republic was established.

to Kagan – it was an unprecedented spectacle for Central Asia when more than a dozen airplanes were concentrated in one place. In addition, a Voisin reconnaissance plane was brought from somewhere. The aviation of the Turkestan Front was commanded by V.Yu. Yungmeister. In accordance with the then accepted system of syllabic abbreviations he was called *nachvozdukhturk* (Head of the Aviation of the Turkistan Front).

The first combat mission was conducted on the morning of 29 August – the 43rd Air Unit carried out the strikes against the enemy. During the day, eight aircraft made 16 reconnaissance and bombing flights, and the crew of N. Fausek hit the Emir's palace

4
AND THE *BASMACHI* AGAIN

The slowdown in the struggle against the *Basmachi* was only temporary. By winter the remnants of the gangs had gone into the mountains to wait out the cold. In the spring of 1921 they returned to the valleys, replenished their ranks with people who were unhappy with the Soviet authorities and resumed their raids and looting.

The troops of the Turkestan Front, Special Operation Units of the State Political Administration, border guards, police and volunteer units of local residents were involved in fighting against the *Basmachi*. Their combined numbers significantly exceeded those of the enemy. The troops were equipped with vehicles, artillery, armoured cars and aviation. However, the effectiveness of their activities was greatly reduced by the challenging terrain and almost a complete lack of roads. There was only one railway and no paved roads. Much of Central Asia was covered by mountains and deserts, making movement of troops difficult and causing logistics problems. The only telegraph line went along the railway tracks, the radio communication did not work well in the mountains; instead, 'walkers' – local peasants worked as messengers, who had to walk many miles for a small reward allocated from the 'Anti-*Basmachi* funds'.

Under the circumstances extensive use of aviation seemed quite natural. But the army of the region operated only two understaffed air reconnaissance units (the 18th and 25th), equipped with various types of two-seater aircraft. According to the regulations at the time, a unit was supposed to have six aircraft in its strength, but it was impossible to find that many. In addition, the air units operated more than one aircraft type, and even then for more than one purpose: both fighters and reconnaissance. Operating fighter airplanes was obviously pointless, as the enemy had no aviation. Since the Turkestan Front was considered secondary, it received only Category 3 equipment – worn out and obsolete.

Moreover, after concluding the treaty with Afghanistan on 28 February 1921, the Turkestanies were required to hand over 12 airplanes to the Afghanis but there was no real possibility of finding them and they offered eight Lebed XII biplanes which were stored in Tashkent, but in good working condition. This type was a replica of the German Albatros aircraft, equipped with different captured German engines, and which were built during the First World War at the Lebedev factory. The question took a long time to solve, and eventually, the Afghanis were allocated one 1½-Strutter, one Nieuport 24 and one Farman 30; the latter crashed during a test flight on the Soviet territory near Termez.

Both the 18th and 25th Air Units were based in Tashkent in winter, with two additional landing grounds available in Askhabat (Ashgabat) and Samarkand. The hostilities continued on a seasonal basis. In winter the *Basmachi* either

Personnel of the 43rd Air Unit near Farman 30 airplane at the airfield in Tashkent.

Flight crews (right to left) A. Eizner, Yu. Beneskriptov, F. Likhovitskiy, unknown, near a Nieuport fighter, Tashkent airfield, 1923.

A disassembled Sopwith 1½-Strutter transported on carts to Afghanistan.

fled to their native villages, stayed somewhere in remote areas, or went across the border to Iran or Afghanistan. In spring they would return 'on the warpath'. When the number of bandit attacks exceeded a certain level, the army would act, with infantry, cavalry and later mechanised units moving into the raided areas, supported by aviation. This pattern of operations had been followed practically since the establishment of Soviet authority in Central Asia.

The *Basmachi* were active in Fergana where the Soviet power was primarily concentrated in the towns and along the railway line. The troops operating there were supported by the 18th Air Unit based in Skobelev, which had only two or three operational aircraft. The unit conducted reconnaissance, directed cavalrymen to the enemy, bombed and fired at the *Basmachi* with machine guns.

At the end of August 1921, all serviceable aircraft of the Turkestan Front were concentrated at Skobelev. There were only eight of them: three Sopwiths, two Nieuports, two Farmans and one Voisin. The new *nachvozdukhturk*, K.N. Bornemann, was in command. The troops were immediately challenged by inaccurate maps or their complete absence, so the pilots photographed the Aravan–Iski–Naukat mountain road as well as the passages among the reeds and swamps near the Syr-Darya River.

At the beginning of the autumn of 1921 three large gangs led by Enver Pasha (a Turk by nationality), Junaid Khan and Kurshermat controlled a considerable part of the territory in the Bukhara Republic. In the vicinity of Fergana, the most powerful leader was Kurshermat; his real name was Mohammed Bek Gazi and his father had once served as vizier of the Kokand Khan. Because of an eye disease that he had suffered in his youth, Muhammad Bek always wore dark glasses and got the nickname 'Kurshermat' – 'Blind Shermat'. His detachment included up to 1,500 Uzbek and Turkmen horsemen.

Since there were few aircraft available, they were organised into flights or even operated individually. For example, the Turkestan Front units at Tejen in October 1921 were supported by just a single aircraft. It conducted reconnaissance missions, occasionally fired at the enemy on the ground, but mostly served for communication. Pilots monitored the movements of the *Basmachi* and attacked their camps. The reconnaissance data was transmitted to the troops on the ground by dropping message streamers.

Kurshermat on a horseback and with a rifle poses for a photographer.

At the beginning of November, the troops launched an offensive against Kurshermat's gang operating in the area between Kokand, Namangan and Andijan. The *Basmachi* were hiding in dense reed thickets, when the aircraft of the 18th Air Unit conducted reconnaissance from the air. Usually, an observer would drop a small bomb in a suspicious place and if the *Basmachi* were there, the explosion caused panic among the horses, giving away the location of the enemy. The crew would return to their airfield and, by waggling the wings, would call for help – the planes on duty were ready to take-off. Then all together they would bomb and shoot at the enemy, and then by dropping message streamers would direct the cavalrymen there.

Small bombs were also used to set dry reeds on fire in an attempt to drive the enemy into the required direction. One 1½-Strutter made a forced landing on a salty patch of land in the reeds near Namangan

Pilots of the 43rd Air Unit, summer 1921.

A DH.9 aircraft of the 4th Air Unit.

A Sopwith 1½-Strutter returns to Kyzyl-Tepe airfield from a reconnaissance flight, 1923.

During this campaign the first night bombing mission was conducted. Three airplanes, piloted by Chernyy, Nikitin and Peregonov struck the *Basmachi* camp near Takali in the dark. They landed at their airfield directed by the light of fires.

Kurshermat's unit was never captured due to the practice of making an agreement with some of the gangs against others. The unit, which had allegedly defected to the Reds' side, defected again and let Kurshermat out of the encirclement. He withdrew to East Bukhara and sat out there until the beginning of the following year.

In November 1921 the cunning Junaid Khan signed a new peace agreement with the government of the Khorezm Republic. In fact, he simply lay low for a while, waiting for an opportune moment.

In the spring of 1922 over 200 Basmachi detachments were detected in the Fergana region. Enver Pasha became the most dangerous enemy and had gathered several tens of thousands of men under his banner. The Fergana group of troops supported by aviation was deployed against him in June. 'Aviation' in this case is, of course, quite an overstatement. There was a single aviation unit, and not all of its airplanes were in serviceable condition.

In April Junaid Khan resumed his actions but did not last long – as early as mid-May some of his *kurbashi* began to negotiate with the

due to engine failure. The machine gun was removed from the aircraft and buried in the sand. Pilot S.N. Nikitin and observer M.V. Bronnikov reached Namangan safely, while the *Basmachi* looked for the aircraft but failed to find it. It was discovered two days later from another airplane, repaired and evacuated. The crew, consisting of pilot P. Peregonov and observer F. Grab, made an emergency landing in the desert. The pilot went with a message to the friendly forces, while the observer stayed behind to guard the aircraft. This time the *Basmachi* spotted the airplane; they captured and beat Graba. However, he was lucky and the Red cavalrymen arrived causing the *Basmachi* to flee and leave their prisoner behind.

A DH.9 assembled in Russia with Mercedes (Daimler) engine at one of the airfields in Central Asia, 1924. Note the Hazet-type radiators on the sides of the fuselage.

Fuel has been brought to the frontline airfield. Pilots rejoice at the opportunity to take-off again.

One aircraft operated in August in eastern Bukhara. By the end of the season one flight was stationed near Samarkand, the other was deployed to west of Bukhara, where the Red Army was chasing detachments of Mullah of Kandahar and Juramin Khan. There the aircraft not only fired machine guns but also dropped small fragmentation and high-explosive bombs.

Then, a detachment of DH.9A biplanes with Liberty engines were deployed from Moscow to Central Asia. The aircraft proved to be very difficult to operate – the engines overheated in the hot climate, and the airplanes often nosed over on soft sandy landing grounds. Only a few full-scale missions were conducted, including the one with a successful bombing near Gissar. Then a fire at the unit's base destroyed all equipment except one aircraft.

In the season of 1923, the *Basmachi* became even more active. They moved quickly, evading the pursuing troops. This called for a more intensive use of aviation. The 4th Reconnaissance Air Unit of six aircraft, which provided support of the Bukhara group of troops, was deployed near Kyzyl-Tepe station in April. On the night of 5 May 1923, communication with the nearest station of Kermene was interrupted. At dawn a watchman made it to the pilots and told them that the station had been attacked and all servicemen who defended it had been killed. The head of the station and the telegrapher were also killed and the building was burned down.

Three airplanes flew out to search for the bandits, and pilot N. Starodumov spotted a detachment of around two hundred horsemen on the route to the mountain pass. After his return to the base, the entire unit flew to the identified target. The airplanes made several approaches in line astern formation, first dropping bombs and then firing machine guns at the enemy. The gang suffered heavy losses. The 8th Air Unit also acted against the *Basmachi*. Pilot P.M. Zakharov and observer A.P. Eisner spotted the enemy in a narrow gorge and dropped bombs right on them. The gang was forced out of the gorge and attacked by the cavalry.

However, not every mission went as smoothly. On 27 November the crew of the 4th Air Unit, consisting of pilot S.I. Baskakov and

Red Army and later surrendered. The gang leader fled to Iran with 120 horsemen.

In January 1922 one aircraft was operating near Ilotan station, and in March of the same year a flight was operating near Karshi. At the beginning of summer, the Bukhara group of troops under the command of N.E. Kakurin started active operations against the *Basmachi*. In June 1922 a flight of four airplanes – two Nieuport fighters and two 1½-Strutters, was sent to southern Bukhara to help. The aircraft were delivered to Karshi, assembled there and ferried further by air. One Nieuport managed to reach Termez, the Sopwith made it to Derbent. From there they tried to conduct reconnaissance missions and attack the *Basmachi*, but the distances were too long for a fighter, so only the 1½-Strutter was in action. It conducted reconnaissance flights and fired machine guns at the enemy.

observer Y.V. Shnitnikov, had to make a forced landing near Lake Makhan due to engine failure. They were attacked by the *Basmachi* of Jura Alim and shot back for two hours. Baskakov was killed, Shnitnikov kept firing from a machine gun, then from a revolver, killing himself with the last bullet. Their bodies were burned together with the plane.

Enver Pasha was defeated and withdrew with the remaining forces to the Afghanistan border. However, he did not make it there himself as he was killed in a clash on 4 August. After that, the enemy's activity gradually decreased and practically died out by the end of 1923. Once again defeated, in November Junaid Khan and the rest of his gang crossed the border of Iran.

Wear and tear as well as accidents dramatically reduced the air fleet of the Turkestan Front. Moreover, the types of aircraft available there were hopelessly outdated. Replenishment was sent from the European part of Russia. However, it was no longer Russia alone – on 30 December 1922 all socialist republics joined the Union of Soviet Socialist Republics (USSR). In Central Asia there were the Kyrgyz (in the north), Turkestan (in the south), Khorezm and Bukhara republics, which were part of the RSFSR as autonomous republics. Together with Russia, they became constituent parts of the USSR.

In April-May 1922, the Soviet Union purchased two dozen LVG VI reconnaissance aircraft from Germany, and most of them ended up in Central Asia. Those airplanes were not new however: they had been manufactured at the end of the First World War. The Turkestan Republic also received some DH.4 biplanes with Italian FIAT engines, which were built in Moscow under the license. These aircraft differed from the British original by the installation of Hazet-type radiators on the sides of the fuselage. However, all that equipment was not enough to improve the quality of the air fleet in general.

5
MILITARY SERVICE OF *DOBROLYOT*

In 1922, transport aviation began to be used for the first time in Central Asia. In order to accelerate the delivery of people and small cargoes, the headquarters of the Turkestan Front opened an air route from Tashkent to Vernyi (later called Alma-Ata, now Almaty). Since there were no specialised aircraft available, old reconnaissance airplanes were used: Farman 30, 1½-Strutter and a captured German Albatros. The distance was 800 kilometres with two intermediate stops, and the flights were made irregularly, with airplanes carrying mail, passengers and cash.

A little later a decision was made to use aircraft from the civil air fleet to support combat operations. The USSR at that time had three airlines that were joint stock companies: *Dobrolyot*, *Ukrvozdukhput* (also referred to as *Ukrpovitroshlyakh*) and *Zakavia*. The latter two companies were engaged in local transportation in Ukraine and Transcaucasia. At the end of 1923, the Central Asian branch of the *Dobrolyot* company was established. A.N. Afanasyev, head of the Air Force of Turkestan Front, was included in its leadership and was appointed a representative of the Main Inspectorate of the society. By 1 January 1924 the branch had received five new Ju-13 airplanes.

In Russia this designation was used for a German Junkers F.13 single-engine all-metal monoplane. The aircraft was considered durable and reliable, but its performance capabilities were quite medium. The airplane was designed for a crew of two (a pilot and a

Chief of a Turkmen tribe Yakshi-Geldy (in the centre) near one of the Ju-13 aircraft of *Dobrolyot* at an airfield in Khiva, spring 1924.

A Ju-13 passenger airplane s/n 713 reg/n R-RDAZ with inscription *Pischevik* (Worker of the food industry) is loaded on a railroad platform. Soon this aircraft would join the Central Asian branch of *Dobrolyot*.

Dobrolyot Ju-13 s/n 712 reg/n R-RDAY *Krasnaya Fergana* (Red Fergana).

Dobrolyot Ju-13 s/n 652 reg/n R-RDAK is prepared for flight, Termez airfield.

flight engineer) and four passengers, while instead of the latter, the aircraft could take up to 350kg of cargo. Without a flight engineer and after removing the seats in the cabin, the payload could be increased to 450kg. The military wanted to have their own transport aircraft, so with the consent of the *Dobrolyot* management, three Ju-13 airplanes were transferred to the Air Force. Two air units received one each, and the Directorate of the District Air Force operated the third one. All these aircraft were considered supernumerary, as the Air Force structure of the time did not include transport airplanes in air units.

The fleet of *Dobrolyot*'s Central Asian branch was restored and even increased with the delivery of both new and used Ju-13s from the European region of the country. In particular, the aircraft and crews from the recently closed Moscow – Nizhniy Novgorod air route were transferred to Central Asia. By January 1925, in Tashkent, which was then the main base of the *Dobrolyot* branch, there were as many as eight aircraft; by July of the next year their number went up to 10. By the spring of 1924 repair workshops and three hangars were built for civil aircraft in Tashkent. In keeping up with the traditions of the time, all airplanes carried their own names inscribed on the nose part of the fuselage, such as *Krasnaya Fergana* (Red Fergana), *Bukharskiy Khlopkorob* (Bukhara Cotton-maker), *ODVF* (abbreviation of the Society of Friends of the Air Fleet), *Irrigator,* and *Upsyrzag* (abbreviation from *Upravleniye Syryevykh Zagotovok* – Department of Raw Materials Procurement).

At first, the Ju-13s made only occasional flights, mostly following orders from local authorities and the military. In the spring of 1925, the Tashkent – Alma-Ata air route was launched, with flights made twice a week starting from 1 May. In July, the Kagan (Novaya Bukhara) – Termez air route followed. Landing sites in the areas of *Basmachi* activity were guarded by the Red Army, the rest were secured by the local police.

Transportation under the Air Force orders was performed under an agreement between *Dobrolyot* and the People's Commissariat for Military and Naval Affairs. Usually only special flights were conducted; however, on occasion the District Air Force authorities would lease a civil aircraft together with its crew for a period of time. Aviation was used to provide supplies to remote border forts and outposts, and to the forward units on the march in inaccessible terrain. Among the passengers there were usually commanders of different ranks, technicians and doctors. Sometimes the airplanes were used to explore the areas of forthcoming military operations or the routes for the troops on the move. Aircraft also were used to carry the sick and wounded.

Given the challenging conditions of Central Asia, the fares for transporting people and cargoes were clearly artificially low; however, the losses were more than offset by direct state subsidies calculated per passenger-kilometre and per tonne-kilometre. Including the subsidies, the Central Asian branch of *Dobrolyot* generated up to 30 percent of profits.

There was no clear division of functions between the military and civil Ju-13s. The *Dobrolyot* crews also flew reconnaissance missions, delivered supplies to combat areas, and provided assistance to pilots who made forced landings. Since the area of operations was considered dangerous, crew members carried revolvers and rifles in case of a forced landing. The *Basmachi*, who had no serious air defence, posed no threat to aircraft. Much more danger was caused by the mountains and the desert with their difficulties of orientation, lack of prepared landing sites, dust storms and strong winds. It was those factors that contributed to the rather high accident rate. However, until 1926 aviation did not play a significant role in the military transportation – animal-drawn transport prevailed everywhere, with assistance of insignificant number of motor vehicles.

6
REORGANISATION AND MODERNISATION

By the mid-1920s the Soviet military structure in Central Asia had undergone some reorganisation. Already in October 1922, four Turkestan divisions located there (1st, 2nd, 3rd and 4th) were reorganised into the 13th Infantry Corps (written as the 'XIIIth Corps' at the time). In 1924 air units of the Turkestan Front were at last manned completely, but the equipment remained outdated.

In total there were four Air Units: the 2nd, 4th, 8th and 11th which operated German LVG C.VI and British DH.9A reconnaissance airplanes, but also operated some older aircraft remaining after the Civil War. It was believed that fighting against the *Basmachi* required nothing particularly modern. In June 1926 the Turkestan Front was transformed into the Central Asian Military District (CAMD).

The state structure also underwent changes. In October 1924, national borders were demarcated – new entities replaced the Turkestan, Bukhara and Khorezm republics. Uzbekistan and Turkmenistan became republics of the Union. Kyrgyzstan first emerged as the Kara-Kyrgyz Autonomous Region of the RSFSR and was simply referred to as Kyrgyz Region starting from 1925. However, it was transformed into a republic of the Union in 1926. Until 1929 Tajikistan was considered an autonomous republic, part of Uzbekistan, and then it also became a republic of the Union. Kazakhstan was the last to achieve this status – until 1936, it was an autonomous republic within the RSFSR. All of those entities remained multi-ethnic but with the prevalence of one ethnic group.

Military operations in the mid-1920s followed the 'occupational' scheme. The units were assigned their own 'occupation zones' where they located small garrisons in

Family members of the crews near a Ju-13 at Tashkent airfield, July 1924. This is one of three aircraft transferred from *Dobrolyot* to Air Force of Central Asian Military District.

Delegates of the 1st Congress of the representatives of the Soviet power in front of the *Dobrolyot* Ju-13 s/n 653 reg/n R-RDAC *Bukharskiy Khlopkorob* (Bukhara Cotton-maker), Dushanbe airfield, Tajikistan, 1924.

settlements. Having surrounded the *Basmachi*-controlled area with those zones they gradually began to tighten the ring. The role of aviation was mainly limited to reconnaissance and communication. The short-range airplanes were deployed to the frontline landing sites which were poorly supplied with caravans of donkeys and camels. They constantly suffered from a shortage of fuel, oil, ammunition and, often, water. As a consequence, the number of flights was relatively low (although much higher than in the districts of Central Russia).

When approached by the Red Army, the *Basmachi* scattered and tried to flee out of the encirclement. It was difficult to distinguish a gang member from a local peasant because, firstly, they were the peasants themselves and, secondly, because the 13th Corps was completely unprepared for local conditions. It was staffed mainly

by conscripts from Ukraine who knew neither the language nor the terrain, while the armament and uniform of the Red Army initially did not differ from those used in the middle part of Russia. Later the uniform was made of lighter fabric for Central Asia, and the soldiers' heads were covered with pointed hybrids of *budyonnovka* (a pointed fabric helmet worn by the Red Army soldiers in 1918–1921) and sun-hats.

For the new power, it was impossible to rely on local authorities, as they were recruited mainly from the more or less literate residents, while only the children of the *Bai*s (local landlords) and the mullahs could read and write. Having taken up a post, those chiefs would first assemble a gang and start collecting tribute from their subordinate tribesmen. The head of the operational department of the CAMD headquarters once wrote in his report:

All the *predispolkom's* (chairman of the executive committees) had created their gangs. Sometimes those people turned from allies into adversaries; a case is known when a large gang was commanded by the chairman of a district executive committee. In another district, after examining the bodies of killed enemies, the servicemen discovered that the dead *kurbashi* was the head of the local police who wore a uniform and insignia.

Therefore, the efficiency of military operations was not very high – the units would complete their mission in one place and then immediately had to relocate somewhere else. In fact, the Soviet authorities had firm control only over the cities and parts of the so-called 'belt of settlement'. The huge sparsely populated areas belonged to no one and lived according to their own rules and laws, often completely unaware that the Tsar had long since been overthrown and replaced by some *Bolsheviks*.

In January 1924 a real uprising broke out in Khorezm. Gangs led by Junaid Khan, who had returned from Iran, and Agaji Ishan seized a considerable part of the territory. At the end of the month, they were joined by Ahmed Bek, so altogether they had about 4,000 horsemen. On 25 January, a 100-man mob attempted to seize the USSR representative office in Khiva, but the guards held the defence of the building. On 27 January the *Basmachi* attempted an assault on Khiva but failed. The 4th Cavalry Regiment, a flight of two aircraft (one DH.9A and one 1½-Strutter) commanded by Y. I. Arvatov and one Ju-13 of *Dobrolyot* were dispatched to help the garrison. Only the Junkers made it safely to their location in Khiva. The Sopwith flown by pilot Likhovitskiy made a forced landing due to engine failure and was lost in the crash. The other two aircraft flew into heavy fog and had to land on the sands 40km west of Pitnyak. The De Havilland piloted by Arvatov ended there. Due to an engine malfunction on landing it struck the wing, fell and flipped over. The aircraft was beyond repair, so the machine gun was removed and the remaining wreck was abandoned. The pilot of the Ju-13 Otto Wiprich (a German citizen, working in the USSR on contract), took on board the crew of Arvatov. On 1 February the Junkers landed in Khiva.

From there Wiprich made one combat sortie, conducting reconnaissance and bombing. However, a single airplane could not have a serious impact on the course of hostilities, so the besieged requested additional assistance. By 20 February eight more aircraft, including five DH.9A and one Ju-13, had been deployed to Khiva. This group was led by the new Head of the Turkestan Front Air Force, P.Kh. Mezheraup.

Three aircraft were stationed in Kunya-Urgench (now Keneurgench) and the rest in Khiva. Aviation provided great assistance in the seizure of the Khanka fortress and in one case, a reconnaissance pilot spotted a cavalry squadron in the desert, which was repulsing the outnumbering *Basmachi*. The pilots came to the rescue and dropped ammunition and medical supplies, and even fired at the enemy.

The airplanes conducted reconnaissance missions, repeatedly discovering gangs of different size and scattering leaflets over the encampments. On 19 March, Mezheraup led five aircraft against Junaid Khan's gang which was spotted south of Lake Tuz-Sultan. The pilots dropped bombs on the riders and tents from a height of 500m, then started shooting at them from machine guns. There was practically no return fire, and the enemy began to wave white flags. At that time a cavalry group attacked and completed the defeat of the *Basmachi*. However, Junaid Khan himself and some of his fighters managed to flee to Sardyvar. They were found two weeks later in the ruins of the Bestemshakh fortress and bombed. On the way back, Mezherup's group were caught in a sandstorm, so only two airplanes out of five made it to Khiva – Mezheraup himself and Lusis. The other three crews landed where they could find a spot, waited out the bad weather and later returned to Khiva.

Successful operations of Soviet forces led to the surrender of the remnants of Agaji Ishan's band including himself. Junaid Khan kept retreating, constantly losing his men and by mid-April he had no more than 25 horsemen left.

At the beginning of May 1924, almost the entire 4th Air Unit was concentrated at a temporary landing ground near Kyzyl-Tepe station, from where the airplanes conducted flights for about a month. Following a short respite, in September the pilots were called in to support the troops chasing Ibrahim Bek's gangs near Dyushambe (now Dushanbe). Operations were conducted there until the end of November, when Ibrahim Bek withdrew to the gorges near the border. After spending the winter there, he left for Afghanistan in early spring.

Soon the 4th Air Unit was renamed into the 40th, and two air units remained in Central Asia: the 40th and 35th. However, under the new staff structure they were supposed to have 10 aircraft each instead of six. The 35th Air Unit was involved in fighting against Djunaid-Khan for three months. It was written in a report: 'Almost the entire flight personnel had extensive flying experience having taken part in operations against the *Basmachi*...'

The year 1925 started about the same as the previous one, but at last the aviators were given new aircraft. In July, new Ju-21 reconnaissance airplanes were brought from Moscow to Tashkent. Those were all-metal monoplanes of German design built by the Junkers concession factory in Fili (a former suburban village, now a neighbourhood in the western section of Moscow, Russia). The airplane was armed with two machine guns: a synchronised Vickers at the front and a Lewis on the turret at the rear. Actually, there was a possibility to place two machine guns in the rear on a double mount, but due to a shortage of them, only one was placed at a time. British-type cartridges were needed for the Vickers machine guns, but they were not delivered in timely fashion. The bomb-carrying capacity of the aircraft was insignificant and limited to the smallest weights (even 20lb bombs were not allowed to be carried on the bomb racks). Moreover, the airplanes initially arrived without any bomb rack beams at all. The flight range of the type was about 400km, which was not enough for the vast expanse of Central Asia; in reality the range turned out to be even smaller.

All the new aircraft were gifts from various locations. For example, four airplanes (pompously named the 'Squadron named after Sverdlov') were solemnly handed over on behalf of the workers of the Ural region on 14 July 1925. The donated aircraft usually carried corresponding inscriptions on the fuselages (*Peasant of Tyumen*, for example).

However, the available aircraft were insufficient to equip two complete air units. At first, the Ju-21 seemed very impressive – the reconnaissance airplane was stable in the air and very durable. The latter feature was considered very important as the temporary airfields used in summer were in terrible condition. However, later it turned out that repairing the duralumin Ju-21 at the field was practically impossible and generally costly. The aircraft had to be delivered to Tashkent for a shop repair. Moreover, the airplane was slow and had poor manoeuvrability. Its insignificant payload capacity made it impossible to use this aircraft for cargo transportation. The range written in the manual was overestimated, and the actual flight time was considerably shorter.

Wreckage of the Sopwith airplane flown by F.V. Likhovitskiy that crashed during an emergency landing in Chardzhou, January 1924. The pilot sits to the left of the engine with his head bandaged.

Head of the Turkestan Front Air Force, P.Kh. Mezheraup.

In order to accelerate the conversion training of the flight personnel, four pilots (Tumanskiy, Rilskiy, Peregonov and Shkapa), observer Janko and several technicians from an air unit that had already mastered the operation of the Ju-21 were transferred to Central Asia. The Junkers was considered a challenging aircraft in handling – the pilots had to deal with the unusually high landing speed. The monoplane had a longer landing distance than the old biplanes and required larger landing grounds.

The 35th Air Unit was the first to convert to the Ju-21. A.K. Tumanskiy and A.V. Rilskiy acted as instructors. The pilots' high expertise made it possible to master the new equipment fairly quickly and complete the combat training programme without accidents. The combat training course was conducted at Troitsk camps near Tashkent. They conducted bombing (imitated by using sandbags),

fired at ground targets and dropped message streamers. The crews also learned navigational techniques in difficult mountainous desert terrain.

On 30 September two aircraft of the 35th Air Unit were redeployed to the frontline landing ground at Nishan station in Tajikistan, and on the next day they conducted their first combat missions. The tactics were simple – the commander of the unit to which the airplanes were assigned would point his finger at the map and order them to look for the Basmachi in the selected spot. The pilots would take-off and look out for groups of horsemen in traditional robes. If the horsemen tried to hide or disperse, they were shot and bombed. Thus, on 9 October a group of about 50 horsemen was spotted in the Kara-Syrt area; five fragmentation bombs were dropped from the height of 500m, and then the Basmachi were fired at with the machine gun from a Lewis turret. On their return, the crew reported everything seen in the flight. However, the Basmachi fled far away in the time it took the crew to return and deliver the report.

Nevertheless, two days later, three gangs (about 80 men in total) appeared in the vicinity of the airfield, so the Ju-21s took off and began to attack. They dropped 24 bombs in several flights and made the enemy retreat. After the post-flight inspection, it turned out that one of the airplanes had 15 bullet holes from the ground fire. The commander of the 13th Infantry Corps, Y.I. Zyuz-Yakovenko, reported to Tashkent: 'The aviation unit is actively supporting our troops....'

The air unit was supplied with fuel and oil by air. For two weeks one Ju-13 shuttled between Termez and Kabedian (approximately 90km distance) carrying fuel and spare parts. The aircraft was piloted by S.A. Shestakov, the same man who later flew to the USA on the ANT-4 airplane named Strana Sovetov (Country of the Soviets).

Later, Shestakov severely damaged this Ju-13 during landing in Termez where he brought spare radiators. The aircraft could only be repaired at the workshops in Tashkent, but no one was willing to ferry it there. So, for a while the airplane stayed at the Termez

Collision of two Ju-21 airplanes at Dushanbe airfield, May 1926. After a reconnaissance flight, pilot Peregonov missed the runaway, went off to the parking area and collided with the Ju-21 *Uralskiy Rabochiy* (Ural Worker) airplane that was also part of the Sverdlov Squadron.

A Ju-21 with inscription *Tyumenskiy Krestyanin* (*Peasant of Tyumen*) which belonged to the 'Squadron named after Sverdlov.'

airfield. Finally, Alexei Tumanskiy agreed to fly it. His brother, Sergey, who later became a well-known aircraft engine designer, flew with him as the flight technician. The Deputy Head of the Turkestan front aviation, Afanasyev, who had to return to Tashkent urgently, was also on board.

The fuel tanks of the damaged aircraft were causing the major concerns. The impact during the crash made them break through the skin of the wing centreplane and, protruding outwards, they were held in place only by the mounting straps. However, the pilots decided to take their chances. As A.K. Tumanskiy later wrote: '...we took off on a half-dead Junkers... The aircraft was literally creaking and cracking and was about to collapse any moment'. Along the way, the plane was hit by the 'Afghani', a strong wind from Afghanistan, which elevated and drove clouds of dust. Ascending to a height of 3,000m, they were guided by the compass and the sun. And worse, Afanasyev, who was sitting on the right-hand seat and acting as the navigator, dropped the map which was immediately blown out of the open cockpit. The pilots lost their bearings and started to look for the railway line. It had already started to get dark when they spotted a passenger train with illuminated windows of carriages. Five minutes later they managed to land next to the train station.

At dawn they moved on. At Milyutinskaya station the crew had to land again as they were running out of fuel. Afanasyev continued his way by train, and the brothers rushed to get the fuel, but it was nowhere to be found. They bought a barrel of kerosene from a local shopkeeper. The engine started but lost its performance during take-off, emitting smoke and soot. Three take-off attempts failed, and the crew decided to wait for the fuel delivery from Tashkent. Tumanskiy later wrote: 'When we arrived safely at the destination, no one understood how we had managed to fly such a wreck'. After that adventure, the brothers were nicknamed *kerosenschiks*.

From 13 November almost the entire 35th Air Unit (six aircraft) was concentrated in the vicinity of Hassan-Kuli where military operations against Junaid Khan's gangs were being conducted. The unit remained there until mid-December.

The 40th Air Unit converted to the new type on the wing-by-wing order as it operated east of Bukhara throughout the whole military campaign of 1925. One wing would be re-equipped in Tashkent and sent back, and another would be flown in to replace it.

On the whole, aviation support to ground troops remained insignificant, as its capabilities were insufficient to meet the needs of the army. In 1925 military operations were conducted in Karakalpakstan, Turkmenistan, southern Uzbekistan (including around Khorezm and Samarkand) and Tajikistan. And this whole territory was covered by support of fewer than 30 aircraft. Therefore, the available equipment was exploited mercilessly. The flight hours turned out to be enormous.

The situation did not undergo any significant changes in 1926. In Tajikistan, for example, by April the intelligence service had

A Ju-21 airplane loaded on a railroad platform.

counted 24 large and small gangs (380 persons in total, of whom only 250 carried firearms) later joined by the Khuram's gang (140 riders), which migrated from the Babatag area. Later on, some local residents who had been previously captured and amnestied or escaped from prisons, as well as Ibrahim Bek's horsemen, who had crossed the Afghan border, joined the *Basmachi* gangs. They were opposed by 2,160 soldiers and 979 horsemen supported by 186 light and medium machine guns. Those forces were additionally staffed with units of the Joint State Political Directorate (OGPU, *Obyedinyonnoye Gosudarstvennoye Politicheskoye Upravleniye*), local police and volunteers. The latter, however, were not given much credence and they were not allowed to issue firearms at first. From the air, this army was supported by only three airplanes of the 40th Air Unit.

The gangs moved from the winter camps to the south and north-west. The troops tried to block them, but to do so they needed to know the routes of the *Basmachi* and the aviation could help to do it. However, in the field it proved inefficient due to the technological shortcomings and underdeveloped tactics, not to mention the large scale of the operational area, the inaccessible terrain, or the lack of prepared take-off and landing sites. The infantry and cavalry commanders did not know how to coordinate their actions with aviation – they could not set the task competently and specifically and did not know the potential of aircraft. There were no ground signallers who knew how to transmit messages with Popham signalling panels. The pilots were often confused about their location over the terrain, but they had no comprehensible maps to use. They did not know how to pick up messages using grappling hooks, and the Red Army soldiers on the ground did not know how to find a site for them and set up poles.

As a result, during the whole period only four missions of locating the gangs were successful. On one occasion the pilots spotted a large group of horsemen in the Aryk-Wau Mountains and dropped a message streamer to the Red cavalrymen, who attacked and defeated the gang. On another occasion the planes themselves dispersed the gang with bombs and machine-gun fire.

Often the pilots' reports could not be used because they were not specific, but it is hard to blame them for this either. Often the report would have something like: 'Around the location of the letter 'B' on the map a dozen horsemen in traditional robes were seen moving in a single-file formation...'. So, where, who and why?

The pilots suffered no casualties or losses from enemy attacks. In 1926, however, two air units had five accidents and one crash, while the Ju-21s were most often damaged during poor landings. The unit logs are full of notes: 'The plane caught wheels on a clay fence', 'hit a ditch', 'jumped on a bump'. That is how the commander of the 40th Air Unit Sadovnichy described his unsuccessful landing at the temporary site 80km away from Tashkent in his explanatory note: 'I had a landing approach at an angle to the runway. The airplane hopped and jumped up. I missed the pedal move. The plane hit the right wheel and crushed the strut'. But overall, despite the challenging conditions, the total accident rate remained about the same as in the Red Army Air Force in general, with the rate of a little over 150 flying hours per accident.

Gradually both pilots and troops on the ground learned the particulars of 'colonial warfare'. Interestingly, everybody was required to study the experience of British operations against rebel tribes in Palestine, Iraq and India, where combat and transport aircraft were actively used. Some of the tricks invented by the experienced colonisers, who owned much of the globe at the time, were very useful to the Red Army.

Starting from 1927 transport aircraft were successfully used as emergency transport, delivering small reinforcements, weapons and ammunition. That year troops were airlifted for the first time. Three planes disembarked 15 Red Army servicemen near a village that was being attacked. Transport flights were not always successful – on 28 April 1927, the Ju-13 of the 35th Air Unit was to deliver cargo to the border outpost of Shiram-Kuy but the engine started to malfunction suddenly. Pilot A.V. Rilski managed to land on barchans (crescent shaped dunes), and the border guards came to the rescue. The aircraft was repaired and flew back to its airfield.

Civil airplanes were also actively used for military purposes. The role of military transport missions for *Dobrolyot* can be assessed basing on the following figures: in October 1927, 80 out of 131 flights were made on the orders of the district commanders and 2,322kg out of 3,036kg of delivered cargoes belonged to the military. Firearms, ammunition, including small-size bombs and fuses for them, medical supplies, mail, newspapers and magazines, and

Ibrahim Bek, a famous *Basmachi* leader.

Cavalry on the march in the mountains.

A Ju-13 passenger airplane and Ju-21 reconnaissance aircraft at the airfield.

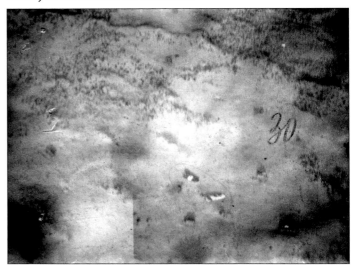

Aerial imagery of the site of the last combat of A.V. Rilskiy's crew; the charred wreckage of the Ju-13 is circled.

Crash of a Ju-21 from the 40th Air Unit, October 1927. Pilot Kovalev, flying from Chardzhu to Tedzhen, failed at landing.

Crash of the Ju-13 piloted by P.M. Zakharov, 1926.

sometimes food were transported by air. In December 1927, for example air reconnaissance spotted several clusters of horsemen 70–80 versts (a verst is a little over a kilometre) westward of Darganat. It was concluded that the *Basmachi* were concentrating their forces to attack the settlement. A *Dobrolyot* airplane delivered 25 rifles and 2,000 rounds of ammunition from Chardzhou to Darganat. Those weapons were intended for a local self-defence unit to reinforce the small garrison and police.

In 1927, the 35th and 40th Air Units fought mainly against the recently returned Junaid Khan in Tajikistan, operating in the area of Kyzyl-Arwat and Tashauz. This cunning old brigand received assistance from abroad which enabled him to arm his men well. Sources write that the British even supplied some anti-aircraft machine guns to his units. The Red airplanes conducted reconnaissance missions, attacked and bombed, while aerial photography became a regular task. Now it became possible to show the commanders the places of future battles, gorges and passages.

Crash of the Ju-21 *Permyak* (*Citizen of Perm*) flown by pilot V. Vasilyev of the 40th Air Unit, Tashkent. The aircraft engine stalled on landing approach, but the pilot could not get to the airfield and the airplane was caught by the clay fence. This Ju-21 was of the last series built and had an enlarged vertical tail. Such aircraft were often recorded as Ju-21A or Ju-21/A.

Pilot E.G. Schakht of the 35th Air Unit near a Ju-13 airplane. Schakht did not originally have a patronymic, it was given to him in the Soviet Union as he was a German-speaking Swiss.

The aerial photos gave an opportunity to evaluate efficiency of the aviation as well.

Combat aircraft were in short supply, and therefore operated with increased intensity. During the summer, each crew flew 300–350 hours, over 100 hours per month. During intensive operations, pilots would spend six to seven hours a day in the air, flying several missions. For modern pilots such figures would seem absolutely unrealistic, but in conditions of non-stop warfare even those were not enough. Therefore, the transport Ju-13s were also used to attack the insurgents. The aircraft were equipped with bomb carriers and simple mechanical bomb release mechanisms. They had no aiming devices, so acceptable accuracy could be achieved only when dropping bombs from low altitudes. Occasionally a machine gun was installed to shoot through a window – sometimes it was an aviation version of the Lewis, but more often a standard 1915 model infantry Lewis was taken. The problem was that the aviation version of the machine gun required special imported ammunition which was always in short supply, while the infantry type could use Russian cartridges from for the 3-line rifle M1891 and Maxim machine gun.

Pilot Rilski, who flew the Ju-13 of the District Air Force, invented his own tactical technique that could now be called a 'mini air assault'. Having spotted a small band of *Basmachi*, he usually memorised the route of their movement. Then he returned to the airfield and took two or three Red Army servicemen with light machine guns on board. He disembarked them on the way of the enemy movement, thus setting an ambush. The airplane took off again and circled nearby. When the enemy ran into the machine-gun fire and was ready to flee, the Ju-13 approached from behind at a low altitude, dropping bombs and firing a machine gun at the *Basmachi*.

Rilski was an experienced and brave man; he flew a lot and performed many successful attacks against the enemy but one day his luck failed him. On 2 October 1927 a gang of *Basmachi* raided the settlement of Khodzha-Kumbez and a messenger who reached the Red Army positions asked for help. The 1st Squadron of the 83rd Cavalry Regiment, supported by the airplanes, moved to help the settlement. Only two aircraft were available at that moment – one Ju-21 and one Ju-13. They attacked the enemies and forced them out of the settlement. The commander of the formation decided to

Crash of Ju-21 flown by Shakht, May 1928. The pilot was found not guilty, as the aileron control cables were mixed up during repair.

hit the bandits once more from the air before they had a chance to disperse, but only the Ju-13 was able to make the second sortie. Trying to drop the bombs more accurately, Rilski violated the order which limited the height of the bomb drop to a minimum of 800m and went down to 200–300m. This cost the entire crew their lives, as the Junkers was met with heavy rifle fire.

During interrogation the captured *Basmachi* later noted that white smoke had suddenly came out of the plane, followed by black smoke, which immediately broke off. The commission investigating the case concluded that the bullet had ruptured the fuel line to the engine (white smoke appeared). The pilot, hearing the bullets hitting the plane, gave full throttle (hence the black smoke) and tried to gain altitude, but there was no more fuel for the engine. This was followed by inevitable forced landing, and the crew faced an unequal fight surrounded by enemies. The pilot, observer and flight engineer were killed.

When the cavalry arrived at the crash site of the Junkers, they found a burned-out aircraft and charred corpses. One of the crew members had been killed or badly wounded while still in the air, his body was discovered in the remains of the aircraft. The other two climbed out and shot back until they were killed. The Basmachi put piles of dried prickly bushes around the Ju-13 and the pilots and set them on fire. The cavalry commander wrote in his report: 'The airplane was smashed to pieces, the wings and airframe burned...'

It should be noted that damage caused to aircraft by gunfire from the ground was quite rare at the time. For example, the aircraft of the entire 40th Air Unit had got only nine bullet holes in the course of two-month combat operations, none of which caused any significant damage.

More frequent trouble was caused by the weather conditions or engine failures. On 17 November 1927, pilot Ya.I. Lepikson of 35th Air Unit took off in his Ju-21 to deliver a secret package with orders to the 3rd Cavalry Unit of OGPU advancing through the sands of the Kara-Kum Desert. Due to poor-quality fuel the carburettor got clogged and the pilot had to land among the barchans. Lepikson knew that about 50km away, near the Sheikh well, there was an outpost of Red Army cavalrymen. He sent an observer there for help, dug a hole under the wing and took up a defensive position with a Lewis machine gun taken off the turret. The pilot did not sleep for 24 hours so as not to be taken off-guard. He decided he would sit in the hole until help arrived or he ran out of water. Lepikson was lucky:

the cavalrymen arrived the next day. Almost immediately after them an airplane arrived that had been sent to look for the messenger. E. Schakht (an active service commander of the Red Army Air Force, but with a Swiss passport!) flew this plane: he picked up the secret mail and delivered it to its destination.

In November 1927 Junaid Khan once again took refuge in Iran. After that he did not risk crossing the Soviet border for several years, but his son and other *kurbashi* continued their raids. They never stayed long in Central Asia; as soon as the Red Army troops started to pursue them, the *Basmachi* left the country. Junaid Khan commanded his men first from Iran and then from Afghanistan.

7
SPECIAL OPERATIONS AIR GROUP

As soon as the Soviet aviation received the first, still-prototype, samples of chemical munitions, they were immediately put into action. The first and only real use of chemical weapons by the Red Army Air Force occurred in the late 1920s. In the spring of 1928, a substantial amount of chemical and fragmentation bombs of various types was transported to Tashkent. According to bills of lading, 275 AKh-8 chemical bombs were delivered there, as well as several batches of not yet officially approved for service 16kg and 32kg chemical bombs, and 8kg chemical fragmentation bombs. The casing of a chemical bomb was filled with a liquid poisonous substance. At the time, mustard gas, lewisite or their mixtures were used. The difference between a chemical fragmentation bomb and a conventional fragmentation bomb was that in the former an ampoule of liquid toxic agent was placed in the centre of the bomb.

In April of the same year, a Special Operations Air Group led by pilot Orlovskiy arrived in Tashkent. The group was not subordinated to the Air Force of the Central Asian District and did not report to their commanders, as the group was not part of this Air Force at all and existed separately. The reports of this group, as well as reports

on its combat operations, have not yet been discovered. However, its work can be assumed from multiple related secondary documents.

For three weeks the personnel hurriedly unloaded and then assembled the R-1 airplanes. This wooden biplane was a Soviet version (though not an exact replica) of the well-known British DH.9A aircraft. The R-1 was powered by an M-5 engine which was a metric copy of the American Liberty engine manufactured at the factories in Moscow and Leningrad. Judging by the accident and repair reports, all equipment of the Group was brand new – the year of the aircraft production was recorded as 1927. One of the airplanes was crashed during a test flight on 27 April by the drunken pilot Yakushenko. Interestingly, in his explanatory note he emphasised that he did not consider himself drunk, as he had consumed only half a glass of vodka, a glass of port wine and a bottle of beer at lunch! The pilots in the group were recruited from different units, mainly from the 30th Air Squadron named 'Red Moscow', which was considered one of the best in the Air Force.

Central Asia, always warm and dry, was a perfect testing ground for chemical weapons. The remoteness from densely populated areas and the poorly educated local population were also an advantage

In the late 1920s and early 1930s, the R-1 wooden biplanes were the most mass-produced aircraft of the Red Army Air Force. The photo shows the airplane built by the Taganrog factory in 1930.

DH.9 s/n H5814 of the 4th Air Unit, Turkestan. (Artwork by Andrey Yurgenson)

Ju-13 s/n 713 reg/n R-RDAZ with inscription *Pischevik* (Worker of the food industry) operated by the Central Asian branch of *Dobrolyot*, Tashkent, September 1924. (Artwork by Andrey Yurgenson)

Ju-13 s/n 652 reg/n R-RDAK operated by *Dobrolyot*, Termez, 1928. (Artwork by Andrey Yurgenson)

Ju-21 *Tyumenskiy Krestyanin* (Tyumen peasant) which belonged to the Squadron named after Sverdlov, July 1925. (Artwork by Andrey Yurgenson)

Ju-13 which was flown by pilot P.M. Zakharov of the 8th Air Unit CAMD, 1926. (Artwork by Andrey Yurgenson)

R-1 *Krasniye Khamovniki* (Red Khamovniki region) of the Special Operations Air Group, Tashkent, May 1928.

Ju-21 flown by pilot A. Plakhotnyuk of the 35th Air Unit, Tashkent, April 1929. (Artwork by Andrey Yurgenson)

Ju-21 flown by pilot N. Miroshnichenko of the 40th Air Unit, Syrdaryinskaya railroad station, April 1929. (Artwork by Andrey Yurgenson)

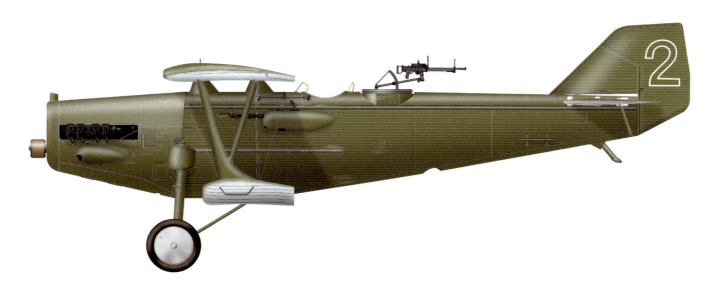

R-3LD s/n 4044 flown by pilot U.G. Bairyshev of the 35th Air Unit, Tashkent, September 1929. (Artwork by Andrey Yurgenson)

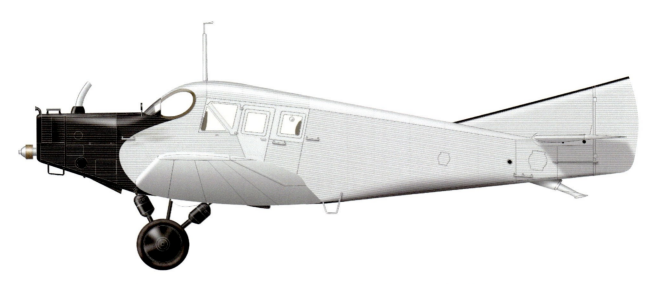

Ju-13 flown by pilot V. Golubev of the Directorate of the 16th Air Brigade, Kulyab, May 1930. (Artwork by Andrey Yurgenson)

R-3LD s/n 4109 flown by pilot S.S. Strelnikov of the 35th Air Unit, Termez, May 1930. (Artwork by Andrey Yurgenson)

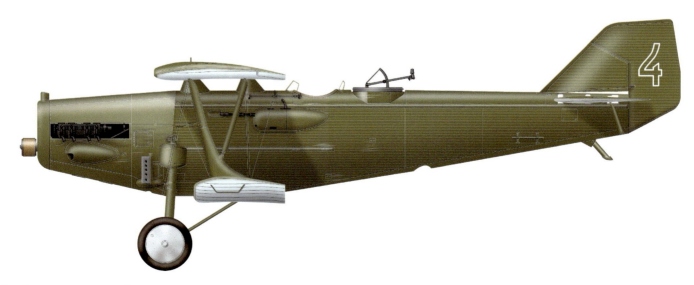

R-3LD of the 35th Air Unit, Termez, June 1930. (Artwork by Andrey Yurgenson)

R-3LD s/n 4084 flown by pilot Kh.Kh. Yangurazov of the 40th Air Unit, Tashkent, April 1941. (Artwork by Andrey Yurgenson)

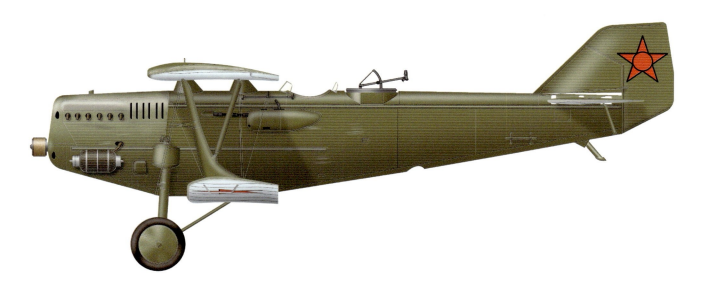

R-3M5 s/n 4001 during tests at the Air Force Scientific Testing Institute, November 1927. (Artwork by Andrey Yurgenson)

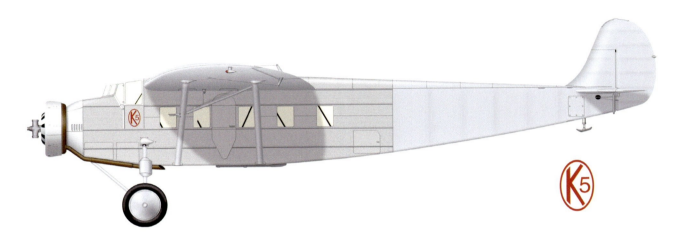

K-5 passenger airplane, February 1932. (Artwork by Andrey Yurgenson)

R-5 of the 1st Air Unit of the OGPU, Tashkent. (Artwork by Andrey Yurgenson)

R-5 flown by pilot L.G. Petrushevskiy of the 37th Squadron, August 1934. (Artwork by Andrey Yurgenson

DI-6 two-seat fighter which was used for ground-attack roles by the Air Force of CAMD, September 1940. (Artwork by Andrey Yurgenson)

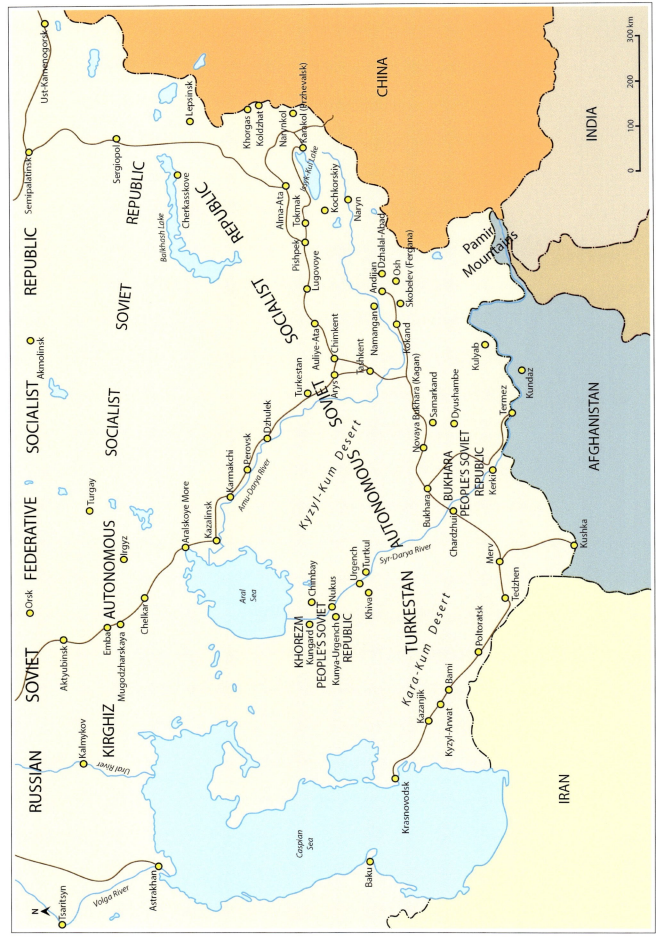

(Map by George Anderson)

One of the R-1 airplanes of the Special Operations Air Group in Tashkent, 1928.

allowing the operations to be carried out secretly. The *Basmachi* had no means of air defence, their machine guns were a rarity and not everyone could even boast a self-made rifle. The locals had never seen a gas mask and did not know what it was for. So it was possible to work within a testing ground, but against live targets.

At the beginning of May 1928, two groups of six aircraft each from the Special Operations Air Group flew from Tashkent via Jizzakh and Samsonovo to Termez. On the way, Orlovskiy lost another aircraft – on 5 May pilot S. Sysoev had to make a forced landing causing his R-1 airplane to nose over and explode.

Soon, the Group's aircraft began to fly combat missions from Termez landing ground. At that time the Red Army and local militias (*kyzyl-askers*) were chasing the *Basmachi* of Junaid Khan in the Kara-Kum Desert. What happened there actually sheds light on the Group's actual mission, and why it was shrouded in a veil of secrecy. On 27 May, a group of seven R-1 airplanes took off, as written in the act, 'to bombard Junaid Khan's gangs'. Hot weather caused the engine failure on the plane of the group commander, V.M. Poray. The plane missed the landing site, hit heavily on the potholes and lost its landing gear. The crew first rushed to check the status of the bombs, suspended under the lower wing. They turned out to be all right: 'Neither fragmentation nor chemical bombs had exploded'.

This DH.9A was used by *Dobrolyot* for aerial survey purposes in Alma-Ata.

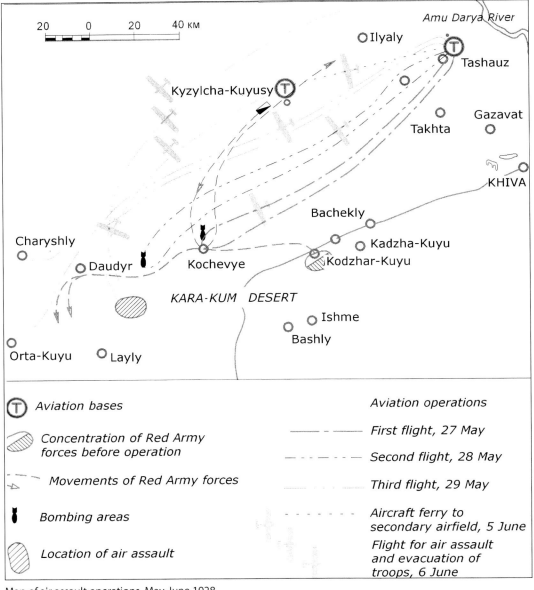

Map of air assault operations, May-June 1928.

almost purely theoretical reasoning. According to it, dropping bombs on bandit groups in open terrain is unfeasible as at the sight of an aircraft horsemen immediately disperse and begin to move quickly. In the mountains, the echo of the working aircraft engine travels very far and immediately betrays the approach of aviation. Under those conditions achieving a killing or even a dangerous concentration of poisonous substance was impossible. Only an attack on villages or camps, where the enemy is taking a rest, can be effective. And even in this case the main victims would be animals, but not humans. However, the headquarters staff considered it to be a good option to reduce the mobility of insurgents and partially deprive them of food. Civil casualties were not a subject of discussion at all.

Apparently, the Special Operations Air Group continued its combat missions until the end of the summer season of 1928. In the autumn the *Basmachi* reduced their activity and withdrew into the remote areas where they would spend the winter, while their opponents did the same. All aircraft were ferried to Tashkent, where they were overhauled and prepared for a new campaign. The Special Operations Air Group is no longer mentioned in the documents of 1929.

The wooden R-1 airplanes did not find an extensive use in Turkestan. Although wood did not deteriorate in its dry climate, all-metal aircraft performed better in the intensive operations.

Two 'local' units, the 35th and 40th, operated in the Tashauz area throughout the summer of 1928, either as complete units or by separating individual wings. At one time there was even a combined wing which included aircraft from both units.

In order to address the lack of comprehensive maps, a systematic aerial photography of remote areas was initiated. A special unit of *Dobrolyot* was engaged in this task. In April 1928 two decommissioned DH.9As were allocated from the Air Force for this purpose. They had a permanent base in Tashkent, but from spring the planes flew to temporary sites for work; and later a third DH.9A was added after repairs.

In November 1928, all aviation units in Central Asia were merged into the 16th Air Brigade, directly subordinated to the Directorate of Red Army Air Force in Moscow.

In the course of further activities, the Special Operations Air Group lost at least one more aircraft. On 12 June 1928, the aforementioned Poray led a flight of R-1 airplanes on a bombing mission from the Tashauz airfield. Immediately after take-off, pilot Batukov and observer Kvade saw 'a solid wall of dust and sand' moving towards them. They lost their bearings in the sandstorm, the aircraft collapsed and burst into flames during forced landing. The crew escaped with bruises only, while the other crews lost sight of each other, but suffered no damage.

In general, the combat aircraft in Central Asia had almost no losses resulting from enemy activity although had a significant number of accidents. The lack of prepared airfields (pilots had to fly from random sites), difficulty in delivering fuel, oil, and spare parts, the remoteness of repair facilities – all this affected condition of the airplanes. The weather was reported to be unstable, with strong upward and downward air currents. Add the heat, dust, lack or poor quality of water – the result would be numerous accidents and crashes.

Orlovskiy's group did provide some information to the District Headquarters. And it explains why his annual report analyses the potential of using chemical bombs against the *Basmachi*. However, the report contains no actual figures or facts, being

8
THE FIRST AIR ASSAULT

During the 1928 season another warfare novelty was used in Central Asia – an air assault. On 27 June a reconnaissance air patrol spotted a group of 50 horsemen and 150 camels with their riders moving towards the ruins of the old fortress of Deu-Kala. They were thought to be one of the detachments of Junaid Khan's gang. The pilots fired at the enemy with their machine guns and returned to the airfield with a report. Two groups of aircraft dropped bombs on the *Basmachi*. Further, the enemy was lost sight of and the air reconnaissance groups returned without results. They decided to look for traces on the ground which would show where the bandits had gone.

A reconnaissance detachment was delivered to the target area by landing the aircraft. The plan was to use four Ju-13 passenger airplanes in this operation, but in reality three were enough. Each airplane carried a pilot, a technician and three assault troopers. The latter were drafted from the command staff of various military units, while the group was headed by the Commander of the 84th Cavalry Regiment A.B. Borisov. The group was armed with two light machine guns and one Maxim machine gun. The area to be searched consisted of several huge sand hollows, separated by sandy mounds overgrown with saxaul. The reconnaissance airplanes found a solid *takyr* (saline area) 2–3km away, but only one aircraft could possibly land on it. Eventually the group decided to land on the *shor*, an open flat sandy area that was spotted 6–7km away.

The group set off from the Kyzylcha-Kuyusy well location. The airplanes with the troopers flew as a group and were accompanied by three Ju-21 reconnaissance aircraft ready to provide fire support. During landing, the wheels of one airplane went deep into the sand, so later this aircraft was barely dragged out to a more solid ground. The reconnaissance airplanes made sure the group landed safely and returned to their airfield.

One pilot, three technicians and a machine gunner with a Maxim stayed to guard the three Ju-13s. The gunner took up a position on a hill, providing good firing area. The rest, divided into two groups of five (each group had one machine gun and rifles) and followed various routes searching the terrain but failed to find anything worth their attention. Four hours later the commander gave the order to return. Meanwhile the Ju-21 airplanes were taking turns circling in the air. They were inspecting the terrain within about 10km off the landing site and were supposed to cover the troops' retreat in case of danger.

In order for the passenger Junkers to ensure their take-off from the soft ground, some of the water had to be drained from them. Two aircraft flew off safely, whereas a magneto failed on the third one, and so one of the Ju-13s later returned with spare parts. After the repairs were completed, both airplanes returned home.

That was the outcome of the first air assault operation in Central Asia. The enemy was not discovered, there was no combat either, but the actual landing and evacuation of the troops with weapons was carried out under real combat conditions. Later, similar operations were repeated several times with much greater success.

9
THE BRAVE AIR ASSAULT OF BRIGADE COMMANDER SHAPKIN

The 1929 campaign was relatively steady, as in most regions only small gangs of *Basmachi* remained. Therefore, the Air Force acted with individual planes. For example, one aircraft interacted with the troops in the Kunduz area and one in the vicinity of Garm. Later, when a small rebellion led by Faizullah Maksum (some documents call him Maksum Fuzaili) broke out in the Tajikistan borderland, one wing of the 35th Air Unit was deployed there. The pilots' tasks remained the same as before: reconnaissance, communications and bombing.

The sources often mention that 45 soldiers were allegedly delivered by six airplanes to repulse the raid by Maksum's gang on the small town of Garm. However, the Ju-13 could carry only six men, a pilot included, not seven as stated in the sources. There were no civil or military aircraft with bigger passenger-carrying capacity in Central Asia at that time. In his memoirs O.I. Gorodovikov, who then commanded the cavalry in that area, described that air assault episode quite differently.

In April 1929 one aircraft delivered five men (three machine-gunners, the Division Commander and his personal adjutant) into Garm, which was under attack by the *Basmachi*. The group was armed with light machine guns and joined the defenders, seriously increasing their firepower. But it was not the machine guns that were crucial for the outcome of the battle, but the diamond-shaped rank badges in the buttonholes of the Division Commander. A former White Guard officer, who was a military adviser to the bandits' leader, supposedly spotted them through the binoculars and concluded that the commander had appeared for some reason, and there should be a large regular part of the Red Army somewhere nearby, which the *Basmachi* would not be able to defeat. He managed to convince the *kurbashi* of that, and his people retreated from Garm. This story of Gorodovikov is much closer to reality than what was written by journalists. However, what did happen in reality?

In mid-April 1929 units of Maksum Fuzaili and Kurshermat seized several villages in the Pamir Mountains and the town of Wanch and then moved on to Garm. A total of about 450 bandits had gathered. There were no troops in Garm so they started mobilising volunteers, while 30 rifles and ammunition were delivered to them by air. The first unit consisted of 18 men: a dozen instructors, three security officers and three Soviet officials; the commander was a bank branch manager. The volunteers encountered the enemy and were all killed. The second unit of seven men entered the battle on the approaches to the town and retreated.

Five Ju-13 aircraft which belonged to *Dobrolyot* and the 35th and 40th Air Units were assigned to perform quick transfer of the reinforcements. The first Junkers of the 40th Air Unit, piloted by N.M. Klochenko, took off in the morning of 23 April. It landed

T.T. Shapkin, commander of the 7th Cavalry Brigade, who led the air assault group in Garm. The photo was taken later, when Shapkin was already commanding the division.

at a site near the town previously spotted from the airplane. The aircraft carried the pilot, the flight technician and there were also platoon leaders Timoshenko and Sergeyev on board. With three light machine guns they, together with the crew, were supposed to defend the landing site. The Ju-13 of *Dobrolyot* arrived at the same site and carried the 7th Cavalry Brigade commander T.T. Shapkin, commissar of the same brigade A.T. Fedin and an unknown platoon commander. The three of them had two light machine guns. By that time the *Basmachi* had already partially seized Garm. Without waiting for reinforcements to arrive, the Brigade Commander led the small squad to attack, and the enemy did retreat. What brought the victory – five machine guns or red diamond rank badges in the buttonholes – still remains unknown. By 30 April aviation had brought 49 soldiers and commanders to Garm, with four machine guns, small arms and ammunition to reinforce the garrison. This time, an armed assault unit (although small in numbers) was disembarked behind enemy lines, encountered the enemy and, together with the forces on the ground, gained victory.

Vyshenskiy's article on the use of aviation in Central Asia, published in the *Vestnik Vozdushnogo Flota* in June 1930, cites the replenishment of remote garrisons as the main task of airborne troops, but states that these forces could also be 'an independent factor'. The main obstacle to the more intensive use of airborne troops was the lack of transport airplanes. Vyshenskiy even suggested that their share in the air units should be increased to half of the fleet.

10
SECRET INVASION

In April 1929 part of the 16th Air Brigade was involved in a secret operation in Afghanistan. The Padishah Amanullah (sometimes also called Emir or King), whom Moscow considered a friend, had been overthrown there. Supporters of the former ruler gathered in the north of the country. Amanullah had summoned about 14,000 soldiers who headed from Kandahar towards Kabul. Soviet troops under the command of V.M. Primakov crossed the border to help them. Those servicemen were drawn from Central Asia and dressed in Afghan uniforms so they could pass as Afghani soldiers. The real Afghanis joined them under the command of General Nabi Khan. Primakov had about 2,000 men in total. They were supported by a group of aircraft from the 35th and 40th Air Units concentrated in Termez. Several Ju-13s of *Dobrolyot* were also deployed there.

On 13 April 1929, six Ju-21s attacked the Afghan border outpost of Patta-Gissar. They dropped several bombs on it, destroying the barracks, and then 'showered' the Afghani soldiers with machine-gun fire. Most of the border guards were killed in the process. The outpost had to be destroyed to ensure an unobstructed border crossing. The first battle on the ground occurred on the same day – the Soviet servicemen encountered a squad moving to help the outpost.

Aviation continuously assisted the Red Army's advance southwards – on 26 April several Ju-13s delivered 10 machine guns and 200 shells for cannons to the Mazar-i-Sharif area. On 6 May the

Probably, one of the aircraft involved in supporting the invasion into Afghanistan. This Ju-21 crashed in Termez on 29 May 1929. Pilot I. Borzin failed to control the aircraft in strong wind during landing.

pilots bombed and fired at the enemy near Mazar-i-Sharif, and on 8 May contributed to the seizure of the Deidadi fortress.

On 22 May, however, Amanullah suddenly stopped fighting and fled to India. For a while the Soviet troops continued acting 'on inertia' supported by aviation. Thus, on 23 May the pilots bombed Khanabad, Andarab, Talikan and Hazrati Imam, and on 25 May they attacked Tashkurgan. On 28 May, A.I. Cherepanov, who had replaced Primakov, was ordered to withdraw to the USSR.

For the sake of disguise, the documents referred to this secret operation in Afghanistan as 'liquidation of banditry in South Turkestan'.

11
CONVERSION TO R-3LD

Weather, poor-quality airfields and unreliable equipment continued to plague the pilots of the 16th Air Brigade. While in the north of Central Asia the steppes prevailed, in the south the pilots had to fly either over the mountains or over the desert. In the mountains they constantly dealt with inconsistent weather and strong upward and downward air currents. All mountainous regions were different, while at the same time there were few reliable navigation points of reference there. Due to the low service ceiling of the aircraft, the pilots flew through gorges, laying complex dogleg routes.

The precipitous cliffs and abundant vegetation made reconnaissance missions challenging. At the same time, the sound of the engine echoed in the mountains, alerting the enemy and giving them time to hide. The pilots were advised to probe the vegetation with machine-gun fire and small bombs. If they noticed movement, it meant that there was an enemy there.

Flying at dawn sometimes helped to spot the traces of the recent camps of the *Basmachi*. If the Red Army servicemen were close, they were alerted and informed by dropping bombs in a certain order, and the direction to the target was indicated by aircraft manoeuvring. Dropping message streamers was also common.

Aviation often supported troops on the ground when the latter were seizing mountain passes and gorges. Shooting and bombing were more difficult in the mountains – targets were often approached at an altitude of 2,000–3,000m, which then had to be dropped quickly. In valleys and especially in gorges, airplanes could not follow a straight course. Free manoeuvring was practically impossible. When planes were climbing away from the target, the *Basmachi* were able to fire at the aircraft from the mountain slopes for up to 10 minutes.

Fighting in the desert was no easier due to the problems with navigation, occasional dust storms that could pull the aircraft to the ground or cause engine failure. A forced landing could only be made on *takyr* (saline area). Airplanes would inevitably nose over when pilots tried landing them on sand as the wheels got stuck. The landing gear of those aircraft types could not be retracted, so landing on the belly was impossible. It was also impossible to take-off from the sand.

As mentioned above, this was aggravated by the unreliability of equipment, especially of the engines. For example, on 18 June 1929 the commander of the 40th Air Unit, P.M. Ivanov, was on a reconnaissance mission near the salty Ser-Oylan Lake. Having

A group of cavalrymen from the OGPU unit.

An R-3LD reconnaissance airplane.

The first accident of an R-3LD in the 16th Air Brigade – commander of the 40th Air Unit P. Ivanov broke the landing gear during landing in Troitsk.

A reconnaissance R-3LD of the 37th Squadron at Tashkent airfield, August 1930.

An additional retractable radiator mounted on the side of R-3LD aircraft was designed in the workshops of the 16th Air Brigade.

Crash of a Ju-13 from the 35th Air Unit at Tashkent airfield, May 1930. Pilot S. Simonenko was supposed to carry passengers and cargo to Troitsk but failed to manage the turn during the take-off.

During a reconnaissance flight, a Ju-13 of the Directorate of the 16th Air Brigade, piloted by V. Golubev, was thrown against a rock in the gorge by a strong wind. With great difficulty the pilot was able to land on a tiny patch of land, May 1930.

dropped the message streamer at the outpost, he turned back, but the engine suddenly failed. During the forced landing, a strong wind blew the aircraft off the final approach. The resulting impact broke the axle of the right wheel and the cabane strut. A Ju-21 airplane from the 35th Air Unit flew out to search for the missing reconnaissance pilot. The pilot, P.M. Mishchenko, spotted the crash site and from the second approach dropped a bag with food for the crew. But then his engine stalled too and the pilot had to make a forced landing. Trying to evade the telegraph line wires, Mishchenko hit a bump and broke the aircraft as well. Both crews had to wait for help from the border guards, who arrived some time later. The end was a happy one, and the cause of both accidents turned out to be contaminated fuel. Such cases encouraged the reconnaissance pilots to fly in pairs as radio was seldom installed on the Ju-21 aircraft. The second aircraft could locate the place of forced landing and bring support.

The intensity of combat missions in 1929 was much lower than the year before. The *Basmachi* were encountered less frequently and mostly in small groups. Sometimes, however, truly amazing things happened. A detachment of the enemy suddenly attacked the field command post of the commander of CAMD, P.E. Dybenko, near Kushka and defeated a platoon of guards. The only aircraft that

Crash of a Ju-21 of the 35th Air Unit, April 1929. Pilot A. Plakhotnyuk departed for a flight from Tashkent to Chinaz, but the aircraft engine stalled after take-off. The pilot struggled to land on the horse racecourse in Tashkent.

Crash of a Ju-21 of the 40th Air Unit during a night landing at a site near the Syrdaryinskaya railroad station, April 1929. Pilot N. Miroshnichenko was delivering an urgent cargo there.

Three R-3LD airplanes of the 35th Air Unit were to be ferried from Tashkent to Tedzhen in September 1929. During the take-off, the airplane flown by pilot U.G. Bairyshev hit a booth with water barrels and crashed.

happened to be on the site nearby helped out. It took off and opened fire with a machine gun from a low altitude. The gunfire and the roar of the engine caused the horses to go rouge and throw the riders off. The attack failed. Then reinforcements arrived. The *Basmachi* tried to flee, but few managed to escape.

Under pressure from the Iranian army, Junaid Khan withdrew to Afghanistan. By the end of 1929 the situation in southern part of Central Asia had become so peaceful that the Commander of the Central Asian District asked Moscow to relieve him of his responsibility for the fight against gangs and hand over all operations to the OGPU.

The relatively low aviation activity was also due to the arrival of new aircraft type in Central Asia. This time they were native R-3LD biplanes, designed by A.N. Tupolev and built at the same factory in Fili, where Junkers were previously made. The new type had an all-metal construction, which had already proven itself in the conditions of the CAMD. The aircraft were equipped with 450hp French water-cooled Lorraine-Dietrich 12Ed engines. Perhaps it was the engines that caused the R-3LD to be deployed to Central Asia. The reason was that they did not start well in cold Russian weather and at temperatures below –20C there were cases of dangerous backfires into the carburettor. In a warm climate it was no longer a problem.

The R-3LD's armament consisted of a directional Vickers machine gun (later series carried a Soviet PV-1) and two Lewis machine guns on a turret in the rear cockpit. Up to 256kg of bombs (up to 32kg each) could be suspended on the carriers under the lower wing. The flight performance of the R-3LD was not impressive at all, and in some respects, it was even inferior to the wooden R-1. The metal plane, however, had twice the durability, which justified its enormous price at the time. The R-3LD cost about 31,000 roubles, more than twice as much as the R-1.

According to the plan of the Red Army Air Force for 1928–29, the 35th and 40th Air Units were supposed to be converted to the new type on a priority basis. Each of them was to receive eight R-3LDs airplanes plus four in reserve. In reality, the first aircraft arrived in June 1929 and they were gradually replacing the outdated types in the 40th Air Unit. After passing the conversion training and completion of the combat training program at the Troitsk firing range, the crews eventually became combat ready. It was at that time that the R-3LD had its first accident. On 13 July 1929, the commander of the 40th Air Unit, P.M. Ivanov, damaged the landing gear when landing at Troitsk airfield.

By autumn, a number of defects had already been revealed in the new aircraft. Aileron bearings burst, fuel cocks leaked and engine mounts cracked. On uneven airfields the wheels deformed, and the innertubes and tyres burst. The main fuel tank rocked in flight, which soon led to fatigue failure of the fuel pipe. The bearings were replaced, the frames were welded and reinforced with steel pads, and the tank was secured with cloth-lined plywood crosses. But most importantly, the engines overheated. Various organisations started to design additional radiators. The first 'tropical' design was suggested by Central Aero-Hydrodynamic Institute. Two diamond-shaped sections were mounted under the lower part of the engine cover. Such radiators were installed on R-3LD at Moscow Factory No.39 before shipping the planes to Central Asia. The radiator worked well but proved inconvenient to operate. It was impossible to remove the lower part of the engine cover without dismantling it. The side panels of the engine cover could not be opened fully as well – again, the additional radiator was in the way. Much more successful was a design invented locally, in the workshops of the 16th Air Brigade in Tashkent. The additional radiator was made in the form of two swivelling sectors located near the landing gear struts. If necessary, the radiators were released into the stream, protruding from the sides of the engine cover like some kind of 'ears'.

The R-3LD received its baptism of fire in March 1930 in the area of Chardzhou and Tashauz, where the gangs of Shaltay Batyr and Rustam Bek were active. Four aircraft of the 35th Air Unit operated there. Not only the 35th and 40th Air Units converted to the new reconnaissance type. After receiving additional airplanes, the 37th Light Bomber Squadron was formed in the CAMD. It was supposed

Participants in the flight Tashkent–Krasnovodsk–Termez–Tashkent near one of the R-3LD airplanes, October 1929.

Unsuccessful night landing of an R-3LD by the commander of the 40th Air Unit Sadovnikov, April 1930.

Crash of an R-3LD of the 35th Air Unit during landing in Termez, June 1930. The crew was conducting a reconnaissance mission along the bank of the Amu-Darya, had to land in the dark and hit a ditch.

to have a full set of 31 aircraft (three wings of 10 airplanes each and one staff aircraft). This made it the most powerful combat air unit in the CAMD. In April 1930, the 1st wing of the 37th Squadron was involved in operations against Kur Artyk's gang in the vicinity of Jilikul. The Ju-21 aiplanes were gradually taken out of operation – the most worn-out ones were written off and the rest were handed over to civil aviation. There was no replacement for the transport Ju-13s yet, so they continued to do their hard work, carrying people and cargoes. They were no longer sent on bombing missions, but still there were plenty of dangerous assignments.

In March 1930, 11 Red Army soldiers and about 60 pre-conscripts that were supposed to be sent to military units were surrounded in the village of Kyzyl-Agach. They had 11 rifles, the same number of sabres, six hunting rifles and a dozen axes. This improvised unit was opposed by several hundred *Basmachi* and took up the defence in an old storehouse, surrounded by two-meter-thick earthen walls.

A Ju-13 from *Dobrolyot* flown by a crew of pilot V.F. Kaminskiy and flight mechanic I.P. Mazuruk (later a famous polar aviation pilot) were sent on a reconnaissance mission. Over Kyzyl-Agach the aircraft was greeted with gunfire. The crew responded with a machine gun and dropped several hand grenades. On the second approach over Kyzyl-Agach, they saw from above that the fighters stretched two white cloths, on which was written crookedly 'No ammunition'. Mazuruk picked up the machine-gun ammunition, wrapped it in his service shirt and dropped it down from a low height. The defenders of the depot held out for another six days until the friendly troops arrived, while the airplane flew in from time to time and dropped ammunition and medical supplies. Kaminskiy and Mazuruk were then each presented with a Mauser handgun engraved 'For the successful fight against counter-revolution from the OGPU board'.

In May 1930 the Ju-13 which belonged to the Directorate of the 16th Air Brigade set off for an aerial reconnaissance mission near Kulyab. The unit commanders of the 7th Cavalry Brigade headed by Brigade Commander Shapkin were on board. The Junkers flew over the gorge through which the troops were supposed to march. A strong gust of wind threw the plane against a rock. Miraculously, the pilot Golubev managed to land on a tiny flat spot. Everyone survived and the plane was even later evacuated and repaired. However, after that incident, Air Brigade Commander Zolotarev forbade reconnaissance flights on Ju-13 without urgent need.

The tactics of ground operations were gradually changing. The approach of so-called 'zones of occupation', which required the dispersal of huge forces, was abandoned. It was replaced by the use of mobile units. The proportion of cavalry in the district was therefore increased, and it was supplemented by motorised infantry on trucks. Each truck carried a machine gun and a Dyakonov mortar (rifle grenade launcher). Entire military units, manned by locals, appeared in the CAMD. Information was provided to the headquarters by the network of agents of the OGPU, which, however, covered only the 'settled zone'. Former exiles proved to be particularly valuable employees, who over the years had learned the local languages, got to know the traditions and customs and made acquaintances among the 'natives'. All this greatly increased the effectiveness of combat operations. In Kazakhstan and Uzbekistan troops were practically no longer involved, as the OGPU managed with its own forces. The *Basmachi* remained only in Tajikistan and Turkmenistan.

12
A NEW OUTBREAK

The situation seemed to be gradually becoming less tense. But in 1931 the Basmachi resumed their raids in Tajikistan and Turkmenistan.

A number of circumstances, both internal and external, contributed to this. On the one hand, Ibrahim Bek's gangs rushed back across

One of the decommissioned Ju-21 airplanes, which was used in Central Asia as civilian postal and aerial survey aircraft.

Captive Ibrahim Bek being transported to the airfield.

Ibrahim Bek near a Ju-13 at the airfield in Tashkent surrounded by militia and OGPU officers.

the Afghanistan border. His *dzhigits* had previously made periodic raids into Soviet Tajikistan, but in small groups. After looting the settlements and encountering the Red Army they would again flee into Afghanistan. However, the Afghan king was fed up with the bandits, who settled in the border areas and obeyed no one. From the summer of 1930 his soldiers moved northward and started to drive Ibrahim Bek out of the permanent encampments. Since the bandits had arrived in Afghanistan with their families and livestock, there was nowhere else for them to go.

Eventually, a lot of people and livestock rushed towards the border. Armed *Basmachi* moved in the rear-guard and covered the retreat. On the Soviet side of the territory the Border Guard units, in particular the 10th Regiment of the OGPU, advanced towards possible crossing points. But Ibrahim Bek outsmarted them. The Reds waited for him to appear near the island of Urta-Tugai for three months and, finally, left. All this time Ibrahim Bek's men were quietly sneaking into Tajikistan mixing together with peaceful refugees. When the troops left the crossing points, Ibrahim Bek moved with a fairly large force (more than 1,500 men) to the other side of the border. More than 6,500 members of their families with their livestock crossed the border with them.

Ibrahim Bek then withdrew to the Jalany-Tau Mountains and began to accumulate forces. By early April he already had around 2,000 horsemen, fairly well organised and armed. Local groups of Kur Artyk (over 300 men) and Ali Mardan (about 500) that had not been annihilated in the previous years had joined them. There were also small local gangs. At Red Army headquarters the *Basmachi* were classified into 'regular' and 'territorial'. The former actively moved from place to place, the latter acted only in their native lands, not moving far from them.

The collectivisation policy pursued by the Soviet government in agriculture had its negative impact. Mass repressions of better-off peasants immediately inevitably served to increase the pool of potential *Basmachi*. Neither were the poor enthusiastic about new policies. The grain confiscated from the people was piled up in dumping points and then taken away while the peasants were allowed to keep the bare minimum. There were cases when local people looted the grain stores and warehouses when the *Basmachi* raided settlements. Food ration cards were implemented in cities, but even they were not enough. The supply of manufactured goods got considerably worse. Collectivisation also completely disrupted traditional trade links. Normally by autumn, nomadic Turkmens would come from the Kara-Kum to the borders of the 'settled belt' and exchange sheep skins and meat for grain, flour, salt, tea and many other goods. Now they got nothing.

Moreover, Soviet officials made ambitious plans for the nomads. They decided that there were too many of the latter in the desert. They decided to keep only small brigades of shepherds there, and to forcibly send everyone else to the cotton plantations as the country needed a lot of gunpowder.

Not surprisingly, all those factors triggered the indignation of the local population. A commission from Moscow, which was sent to deal with the situation, stated quite frankly in its report: 'it is no surprise that the *dekhan* [peasants in Central Asia] go into *Basmachi*, what is surprising is that all of them haven't done it yet'. One member of the commission wrote: 'The only thing that saves us is the oppressed nature of the local peasantry, accustomed over the centuries to the constant abuse of the authorities'.

The 1931 campaign began in Tajikistan. The Tajik Group of Red Army forces was deployed against Ibrahim Bek: a rifle division, two cavalry brigades as well as artillery and motorised units. The commander of the group, I.K. Gryaznov, issued an order stating: 'The infiltration of the *Basmachi* gangs into the territory of Soviet Tajikistan is an audacious attempt of the class enemy to disrupt building of socialism in the Tajik Republic'. The group was supported by aircraft from two air units temporarily combined into the Tajik Air Group led by the Commander of the 16th Air Brigade, I.E. Bogoslov.

The first to arrive were seven aircraft of the 35th Air Unit, which launched the military operations on 27 March. Then four aircraft from the 40th Air Unit and one from Brigade Headquarters arrived. A total of 12 R-3LD airplanes were deployed, later their number decreased to 10. Three Ju-13s which belonged to the Air Force transported tools, equipment, spare parts and ammunition for the aviators to the landing grounds at the frontline. This group was

An R-3LD of the 40th Air Unit after a forced landing near Yanka-Sergay during the flight from Tashkent to Stalinabad. Pilot Kh.Kh. Yangurazov was forced to land due to heavy fog.

Crash of the R-3LD airplane piloted by A.I. Maruzhenko in the ravine at Tamerlane's Gate, 40km away from Samarkand, April 1931.

However, the Soviet troops were also gradually learning how to interact with the aviation. Signallers, who accompanied the forces, laid out coded messages for the pilots with Popham signalling panels – large strips of white cloth. In the absence of cloth, the signs were laid out from horse saddles or created by lining up men. Red Army servicemen marked their location with coloured flares. Urgent reports from the ground were picked up by special hooks: the packet hung on a rope stretched between poles or pyramids of rifles.

The pilots, in their turn, sent messages to the troops by dropping message streamers. Although primitive, this method proved quite effective. The planes began to point Red cavalrymen at the gangs and then support the attack with small fragmentation bombs and machine-gun fire. However, the timing had to be planned carefully to avoid starting the assault too early. On several occasions, when the aircraft attacked, the gangs immediately dispersed and fled in different directions before the cavalry or motorised riflemen had even approached. The 40th Air Unit tried releasing homing pigeons from the rear cockpit and the birds returned to the headquarters dovecote. Dropping leaflets was used to alert the population, but the vast majority of the locals were completely illiterate. Bombs were usually dropped from an altitude of 400m, machine guns were fired from 100m. To enhance the accuracy, the pilots tried bombing from a shallow dive. But the lack of experience resulted in one of the planes being hit eight times by fragments of its own bombs.

supported by airplanes of civil aviation. By August 1931 the Central Asia Directorate of Civil Air Fleet had seven K-4s (single-engine aircraft for two crew members and three passengers), eight Ju-13s, one three-engine JuG-1 (Junkers K.30C) bomber stripped off its weapons, one Dornier *Merkur*, one Fokker C. IV and 21 Ju-21s also without armament.

In the course of that campaign both sides came up with a lot of new things. For the first time the Red Army faced well-coordinated gangs. The authority of Ibrahim Bek united the rebels and encouraged them to fight together. Then, the *Basmachi* learned to fight against aviation. Airplanes no longer intimidated them – whenever an aircraft showed up, the horsemen quickly dispersed, hiding in the shade of rocks, gorges, among trees and bushes. Covert movement of bandits with their herds became very common. If the *Basmachi* were caught by an air strike in the open area, they would open dense rifle fire and they even assigned snipers to shoot at the airplanes. The gangs moved quickly, forcing the Red Army to conduct almost non-stop aerial reconnaissance. In some cases the *Basmachi* hid in villages disguised as civilians. They also used caves where neither bombs nor machine guns could reach them.

The medical service formed a special surgical brigade, which was flown to the site. Wounded fighters were airlifted to Stalinabad (renamed from Fergana in 1929), where ambulance vehicles were on duty at the airfield. The delivery of urgent cargo by air was actively used. The Ju-13s of both the Air Force and *Dobrolyot* were fully engaged. Occasionally, small urgent cargoes were also delivered by combat aircraft. Thus, on 12 April the Commander of the 35th Air Unit A.I. Kalyuzhnov brought to the village of Yavan the cash needed for the supply officers to pay the local population for food and fodder. The Junkers were also used as back-up in case of a forced landing, escorting groups of combat airplanes.

Pilots of the Tajik Air Group sometimes conducted very successful operations. Thus, on 15 April 1931 the aircraft spotted Kur Artyk's gang (of about 300 men) on the crossing of the Kyzyl-Su

Camels were used where trucks and horses could not pass in the sands: A Red Army serviceman rides a camel and leads another loaded with a Maxim machine gun.

Crash of an R-3LD of the 40th Air Unit; the crew of M. Plavelski was flying to establish communication with a machine-gun platoon, but the engine stalled over the Gardani–Ushti pass.

Red cavalrymen lost only one. The gang was defeated – Kur Artyk fled, periodically bumping into cavalrymen or mobile groups in vehicles. The pitiful remnants of his gang hid in the Teregli-Tau Mountains. Another gang, headed by Ali Mardan, came under heavy strike from the air. Three groups of airplanes, taking turns, fired at and bombed it for five hours. Eventually the gang leader ended up sending out envoys and laid down his arms.

Ibrahim Bek also suffered losses. He was trying to reach the Lokai district, where his relatives lived. On the way he managed to defeat the combined detachment of the 79th Cavalry Regiment, which was not difficult considering the tenfold superiority in numbers. But the full squadron of Red cavalry was already out of his league, so the gang began to rush around. The aviation watched its whereabouts non-stop. The aircraft of Wing Commander A. Mitrofanov was deployed to support the cavalry regiment stationed in Kulyab. During the first flight the pilot spotted the *Basmachi* on the plain near the winter hut of Ak-Djar. When the reconnaissance aircraft descended to see what was happening below, it was met with rifle fire. In response, observer Abdurakhmanov fired at the enemy with all his ammunition. Mitrofanov found a detachment of Red cavalrymen and dropped a message streamer to them. Then the crew conducted two more flights, now with bombing. The next day there were three airplanes participating in the chase, and the Red Army soldiers attacked the gang from different sides.

As a result, the *Basmachi* were pinned down to the Vakhsh River. They began to rush along the bank in search of a place to cross. The aircraft were constantly conducting reconnaissance, which was quite difficult in the mountains. The gang crossed the river on goatskins, but then it was driven by the air strikes along the left bank; its numbers kept dwindling.

River. It was chased by the 80th Cavalry Regiment. The *Basmachi* were attacked by nine aircraft which managed to stop the crossing by bombing. The pilots found the location of the Red Army men and led them to the river. Two squadrons of cavalry attacked the *Basmachi*, and the enemy fled. At the battle site 101 corpses were discovered, three bandits were taken prisoner; the trophies included 21 rifles and 67 horses.

Kur Artyk went north but was attacked by a division of the 79th Cavalry Regiment and the Kulyab Volunteer Force. They drove the gang back towards Kyzyl-Su. Two days later Kur Artyk was spotted by pilots 40km southwest of Kurgan-Tyube. His gang was reduced threefold, and the *Basmachi* were moving westwards. With the help of message streamers, a squadron of cavalry and a detachment of motorised infantry in trucks with machine guns were directed against the bandits. Covering his retreat, Kur Artyk threw weakly armed 'stick-men' into a suicide attack. While they were being slaughtered by machine-gun fire, the *kurbashi* and a group of his cronies withdrew. But in the process, he lost over 50 men, while the

Mitrofanov described the assault at Sarsarak Mountain in his memoirs: 'In the heat of battle excitement, not paying attention to the shots of the *Basmachi*, I was descending lower and lower. Sometime later there was not a single rider left on the horses – the bullets scattered them over the ravine'. The group commander reported to Tashkent: 'The group has shown exceptional courage and assertiveness in their work, thanks to which they are terrorising and causing panic among the *Basmachi* gangs'. At the beginning of June Ibrahim Bek managed to break through into Uzbekistan and withdrew to his home Lokai valley. However, only 550 horsemen remained at his disposal, and even they gradually dispersed. In his memoirs Mitrofanov wrote that he discovered a group of 30 *Basmachi*, who had hidden in a ravine, and used machine guns to shoot them. On 23 June Ibrahim Bek came out to the Kafirnigan River with just two *dzhigits* and tried to cross to the other side, but local people, lured by the reward on his head, informed the commander of the local volunteer detachment. The authorities offered a lot: 5,000 roubles and a horse for information on Ibrahim

Bek's whereabouts; 10,000 roubles and exemption from taxes for life for his capture; 100,000 roubles to the village for his extradition. The commander of the group organised the capture of the famous enemy – Ibrahim Bek was delivered to Tashkent on a Ju-13 airplane.

By the end of June the enemy was completely dispersed, some 1,550 *Basmachi* were killed and 2,000 taken prisoner. The Tajik Group of Red Army forces was disbanded as the task was completed. In the course of this campaign the Tajik Air Group flew 268 challenging combat missions in the mountains, dropping 40 bombs and shooting 4,711 bullets. The report later noted: 'Gang hit rate is low'. This was attributed primarily to the rapid dispersal of the enemy.

Pilots also suffered casualties; however, they were caused more by the wear and tear of the equipment and piloting errors, while combat damage was a rare occasion. There were two accidents, one of them due to a ruptured wheel on take-off. Four forced landings occurred due to engine failures; in one case, a broken connecting rod was later identified as a cause. Pilot A.I. Maruzhenko of the 40th Air Unit crashed his aircraft near Tamerlane's Gate while flying to Stalinabad. In the gorge his plane hit a slope. The pilot and a mechanic sitting in the rear cabin were injured. The commission later found that Maruzhenko had not had time to sufficiently master the R-3LD (he had previously flown the Ju-21).

The biggest tragedy happened to pilot M. Plavelskiy from the same 40th Air Unit. His crew was on a reconnaissance mission along the valley route of the Red Army and *kyzyl-askers*. Suddenly a big band of *Basmachi* appeared ahead and met the airplane with a dense rifle fire. The engine stalled – it looked like the fuel line had been broken. However, Plavelskiy landed quite successfully on a mountain slope. He sent the observer with his Mauser gun for help and took up the defence position with a turret machine gun. The bandits got there before the Red Army. The squadron, which arrived at the place of landing at dawn, found only the P-3LD, the metal skin of which was hacked with sabres and axes. The pilot was never found, and where and how he died remained unknown.

Interestingly, the final report of the Tajik Air Group for 1931 suggested using chemical weapons against the *Basmachi*. By that time, the R-3LDs had been supplied with VAP-6 liquid discharge devices. Those were tanks filled with solution of poisonous substances in kerosene. When opened, the pressure of the oncoming air flow displaced the liquid from the tank and sprayed it through a nozzle. The aircraft could carry two of those devices under the lower wing but there is no information about their actual use in the field.

Throughout the spring, there was a growing threat from the nomadic Turkmen herdsmen tribes roaming the Kara-Kum. They raided small settlements and clashed with police and military units. Turkmens proved to be good fighters, disciplined, persistent, and proficient in guerrilla warfare tactics. The Red units sent against them were often ambushed. From April 1931 aircraft were deployed against the Turkmens. Initially, one reinforced wing of the 37th Squadron (13 aircraft) was deployed. Five to seven airplanes were deployed in Kyzyl-Arvat, three to five in Tashauz, one to three in Merv, and one to three in Kushka. Later, the airplanes of the 35th Air Unit were added. The group was commanded by Krestyanov. In fact, there was constant shuffling of aircraft and crews operating in Tajikistan and Turkmenistan. In all, at various times 10 to 18 airplanes were used. From time to time, they were ferried back to Tashkent for engine overhaul.

The first combat mission was conducted by the Commander of the 35th Air Unit, A.I. Kalyuzhnov, on the morning of 7 April, but during the reconnaissance they spotted only grazing cattle. Later

that day the first *Basmachi* were also discovered: about two dozen horsemen were descending into the valley but when the airplane appeared, they scattered. The next day the first bombs were dropped. However, only small groups of up to 50 men were encountered. On 10 April a gang of 200 horsemen was spotted near the village of Shurga, and it was attacked by a wing of R-3LDs.

On 13 April the pilots came under return fire from the ground for the first time – the *Basmachi* fired on Mishchenko and Nedosekin's airplanes. The next day the aviators helped the Red cavalrymen out of trouble. The cavalry group ran into a retreating gang of about 250 horsemen. The Red soldiers would have been cut down quickly, but for the aircraft that came to the rescue. The pilots drove the enemy away with machine-gun fire and bombs.

In Turkmenistan, the same tactics as in Tajikistan were used successfully. On 29 April pilot Mitrofanov spotted a gang resting in the shade of trees on Hasan-Dog Mountain. Using the message streamers, he directed three squadrons to surround the enemy. When the Red cavalry went on the attack, the aircraft began bombing and firing at the *Basmachi*. Their attempt to break out of the encirclement failed. Only half a dozen of the enemy managed to climb a very steep slope, but the gunfire from the airplane smashed them as well.

It must be noted that it was not easy to distinguish the friendly population from the enemy. The pilots often brought back reports such as: 'From the village of Kungi a group of nine men in coloured tunics was moving towards the Yavan River'. The following wording was often used: 'It was impossible to establish whether the group was a *Basmachi* gang or not'. Often the pilots used a 'trial-and-error method': they dropped a bomb and waited for the return fire; if it began, they were definitely *Basmachi*. If they did not fire in return, then who knows...

Turkmen nomads travelled with their families and large numbers of livestock, so it was almost impossible to distinguish between herdsmen and bandits. In one example, from the air the pilots counted 'approximately 200 people' ('the number of horsemen is difficult to count, they disperse and take camouflage measures when an aircraft appears'), and with them – 4,000 sheep, 140–150 camels and... 400 *kibitkas* (covered wagons). Hence the conclusion that only those in plain sight could be counted, and which of them were *Basmachi* and which were not, remained unclear.

The Headquarters' approach was simple – everyone in the gang-controlled areas was considered an enemy (or an accomplice of the enemy). The aviation was given 'free-fire' zones, where no one was considered 'friendly', and the pilots were ordered to shoot and bomb everything at random there. Attacks were made on crowds of people, cattle and housing of any kind. The destruction of livestock was explained, for example, by the effort to deprive the *Basmachi* of food. In addition, bombing herds in some cases really helped to identify small gangs camouflaged among the animals. The pilots phrased it more simply: 'In the sands all nomads are *Basmachi*'. Some hotheads even adhered to the slogan 'A good Turkmen is a dead Turkmen!'. But OGPU agents quickly reported this information to the authorities, and the OGPU officers began intensively brainwashing the flying and technical staff explaining that 'a Turkmen is a human being too'.

In the course of the first period of the 1931 campaign (until 1 June), 307 combat flights were conducted in Turkmenistan, of which only 34 were bombing missions.

13
KARA-KUM CAMPAIGN

Gradually the rebellious Turkmen tribes became the most dangerous enemies of the Red Army in the Kara-Kum Desert. The self-defence units previously formed to fight the *Basmachi* merged with the gangs. From July of 1931 the Turkmen began systematic attacks against military outposts and railway stations. On 12 July Atadjan's gang took Kyzyl-Tepe, defeating a security detachment. On 27 July three gangs (about 300 riders in total) approached the Ak-Kuyu Well and offered to allow the local volunteers who were defending it to surrender. The volunteer unit held out for four days but was eventually defeated. The Red unit sent to help was ambushed. Out of 90 men and commanders, only 17 men with one light machine gun returned to their fellow troops. On the night of 30 July Turkmens seized Kazanjin station and derailed the mail train. There was a four-hour fight with the militia and the OGPU unit, joined by the train's passengers and railway workers. Another detachment of Turkmens raided and looted the Perevalnaya station. The *Basmachi* dismantled the tracks, causing a passenger train to derail. After a series of such incidents, the Soviet leadership began to seriously fear that the nomadic Turkmens would penetrate the 'settled belt'. 'The *Basmachi* gangs operating in the sands have become completely insolent', the Head of the Political Department of the Turkmen Cavalry Brigade reported to his superiors.

The large gang headed by Orazgeldy had already been defeated by September 1931, its remnants scattered, making their way in small groups to the border with Iran; on the way they looted. Akhmed Bek's gang of about 150 men settled near the village of Dohly (40km from Sernyi Zavod station). Two other gangs, totalling up to 100 horsemen, were also operating in the same area. According to intelligence reports, Ahmed Bek hoped to unite all those forces and take the village of Kyzyl-Takir, cutting off Sernyi Zavod from Ashkhabad and Derbent and depriving it of water. A large group of Turkmen Red Army fighters from Koymata put up roadblocks of 100–150 servicemen near the wells: they entrenched there in

preparation for the defence. Their mission was to ensure that the majority of the civil population with their livestock retreat to safety.

The Turkmen aviation group was formed, including a control unit and all combat-ready aircraft taken from the 37th Squadron, and the 35th and 40th Air Units. The airplanes were ferried from Tashkent to Kyzyl-Arvat in two groups with intermediate stops in Chardzhou and Merv. All together there were 28 R-3LDs, one Ju-13, two R-5s and one ANT-9. The latter two types were new. The R-5 was a fairly large wooden biplane with an M-17 engine. Its performance was far superior to the R-3LD with the standard bomb load up to 500kg, but in overload it could carry up to 800kg. Those aircraft were flown by the commanders – commander of the group (he was also Commander of the 16th Air Brigade), I.E. Bogoslov and Commander of the 37th Squadron, I.A. Nazarchuk.

Transferred from the Ukrainian Military District, the ANT-9 was fairly large for its time: a three-engined all-metal transport aircraft. There were nine passenger seats in the cabin, but passengers could also be seated on the floor in the aisle, so up to 12 passengers could be carried this way. If the runway was big enough, the airplane could also carry some cargo. There were not even a dozen ANT-9s in the Air Force, and the fact that one aircraft was allocated to the CAMD emphasised the importance of air transport in that district. Airplanes of the Turkmen Air Group were deployed to frontier airfields, with supply provided mainly by camel caravans. The operations were commanded by Brigade Commander Bogoslov.

In August the Red Army began the Kara-Kum campaign. One group of troops disembarked in the port of Krasnovodsk on the Caspian Sea. It included motorised infantry, armoured vehicles and T-27 tankettes. A wing of the R-3LDs also was ferried there. The ground crews and some of the necessary equipment were transported by Junkers airplanes. From Krasnovodsk the combined mechanised detachment went into the desert, making their way from well to well. Wherever suitable landing grounds were found,

A new R-5 reconnaissance biplane which began to enter service with the Red Army Air Force in the early 1930s.

A three-engine ANT-9 passenger airplane powered by Wright J6 engines; the Red Army Air Force received aircraft with these engines only.

Crash of a Ju-13 airplane flown by pilot V.M. Shnei at the site near the Derbent Well, 10 August 1931.

Similar cases happened almost daily – on 21 August three R-3LDs spotted 70–80 riders at the Nakar-Kuyu Well. They dropped 24 small bombs and shot 1,000 bullets. In his report the commander of the wing wrote: 'A considerable defeat of manpower was detected'. The *Basmachi* also fired back at the airplanes.

On 24 August the R-3LD of the 35th Air Unit crashed while trying to pick up a message with a hook from the ground near Karavikol village. Pilot V.Y. Anderson missed and hit the ground at low altitude. A surgeon and two technicians were transported to the crash site by Ju-13, and the body of the perished observer A.V. Nikolaev was flown back to Ashkhabad.

The main target of the air operations seemed to become intimidation of the local population. Almost half of the bombing missions were directed at encampments where, for every man able to fight, there were over a dozen women, children and elderly people. The reports described it as follows: 'When airplanes appear, all living things abandon the *aul* [a small Central Asian village] and hide in barchans and thickets of saxaul... The number of *auls* and yurts in the area of aviation activities has considerably decreased'. In some cases there were so-called 'demonstration of power' raids – the airplanes simply passed over a village at a low altitude several times. When carrying out bombing mission the pilots also preferred effect to efficiency. They were using high-explosive bombs, which made a lot of noise and dust, rather than shrapnel bombs, which could really injure more people. Airplanes also hunted down caravans in the sands. For example, on 28 August a caravan of 250–300 camels, accompanied by 70 riders, was destroyed near the Gerli Ata Well.

The Turkmen did not just wait on the defensive. On 24 August 1931 one of the gangs attacked the frontline airfield. All 10 men there, including Brigade Doctor Lodziato, took up arms and successfully defended the airplanes. On 26 August 1931, Hakmurat's gang besieged the railway station of Jebel. A group of R-3LDs, led by Kalyuzhnov, flew to the aid of a small group of Red Army soldiers and militia. The airplanes dropped bombs – the crew of Gruzdev suppressed a key position of the *Basmachi* at the water pumping station – and attacked the enemy with machine-gun fire. A bullet hit the fuel tank of Kalyuzhnov's airplane; however, risking exploding every minute, he continued the attack until the enemy began to retreat. Only then did the pilot make an emergency landing.

On 12 September the pilot M.F. Mishchenko was sent with a report to Lomanov, the commander of the mechanised unit. When Mishchenko took off from the unit's encampment, he discovered an ambush of the *Basmachi* a kilometre away. Despite the altitude of just 50m, the pilot attacked the enemy without hesitation. The bandits met the airplane with massive rifle fire at point-blank range, having hit the aircraft twice. The quick-wittedness of the pilot gave time for the motorised unit to deploy in battle formation and crush the *Basmachi*.

the Ju-13s were flown with supply of fuel and oil for the equipment, as well as fresh food and fodder for the horses. The wells which were found along the way did not contain enough water for the big group. Initially it was planned to bring additional water on camels but the process was not properly organised, so water had to be transported by air too. Regular air reconnaissance was carried out, and it became the only method to get operative information about the enemy's position. Aircraft also delivered orders, various documents and maps, as well as fresh newspapers. The sick and wounded (there were seven of them in total) were taken on the return flights. On 10 August the Ju-13 flown by pilot V.M. Shnei, carrying fuel, got into an accident near the Derbent Well. A gust of wind threw the airplane onto a hill; as a result, the landing gear and propeller were damaged. The aircraft was later repaired and flown back.

As early as 14 August, aviation began attacking the rebel tribal settlements. Near the Adji-Kuyu Well the Red airplanes flown from Krasnovodsk spotted five mud-brick structures and about 40 yurts, with camels and horses grazing nearby. The pilots thought it was a 'bandit stronghold' and dropped bombs.

A motorised detachment is waiting for the arrival of a transport airplane at the landing ground near the Derbent Well.

Navigation over the desert remained a challenge for the air crews. On 21 September pilots Shnei on the Ju-13, and Petrov on the R-3LD, conducted bombing missions. Along the way, the crews lost sight of each other and got lost. Schnei landed near a group of locals and tried to find out where he was. He did not know the language, explained himself by signs and continued his trip but got lost again. He landed again and tried to negotiate with people on the ground. As a result, he found the target Turkmen settlement, dropped bombs on it and returned to his airfield.

The mechanised unit of the Red Army had two major battles with the Turkmens, both in early September: at the Tuar camp and at the Chagyl Well.

Crash of an R-3LD airplane of the 37th Squadron; pilot A. Ogurtsov made a mistake at landing near Dzhibela station after the reconnaissance flight.

In both cases the attack was supported by aircraft, although reports say that 'the heavy bombing did not cause panic'. By the standards of the Central Asian warfare, this was indeed a serious blow. For example, Chagyl, which was defended by 600 men, was bombed and shelled for three days by 22 aircraft. Even old Ju-13s and the ANT-9 transport were involved. They dropped 392 bombs (mainly AO-8 fragmentation bombs, 8kg each). The ANT-9 took 80 bombs at a time, working almost at maximum carrying capacity. Even with double-point mounts it was impossible to install such a number of the bomb carriers on the aircraft and apparently, the bombs were simply loaded into the fuselage in a crate and then thrown out of the door by the pilots.

Of course, the nomads could not resist artillery, planes and tankettes. Abandoning their families and livestock, the men retreated into the desert. Among those left behind not a single male over the age of 12 could be found – the teenagers had also become warriors. The losses of the Red Army were minuscule – the Turkmens managed to burn only one tankette that fell into a hidden pit. The retreating rebels were chased by the aircraft, which dropped 150 bombs on their heads. The report recorded: 'The results of the bombing were good'.

Interestingly, the Turkmens, who were considered cruel people, treated the Red Army prisoners well, especially the Muslims. The prisoners were told: 'We didn't want to fight, leave us alone, we just want to live freely'. The POWs were often released, given food and water for the journey. Upon their return, the political officers demanded that the former POWs be isolated immediately and not allowed to communicate with other Red Army soldiers.

Another novelty of the 1931 campaign was the redeployment of technical personnel and equipment by aircraft to the frontier airfield of Ak-Yaydy, where a large part of the Turkmen Air Group was relocated in mid-September.

There was one case of a friendly fire. A unit of the 2nd Cavalry Regiment marched in to assist the garrison at the Derbent Well that was surrounded by the *Basmachi*. Two days later it approached the well and drove the enemy back. Then five R-3LDs appeared and began bombing, not the bandits, but the Red Army men. As Popham signalling panels and signallers remained in the vehicle which was stuck along the road, the Red Servicemen made an improvised 'T' sign and began waving red flags. Despite this, the airplanes dropped the remaining bombs and fired machine guns, so the soldiers retreated to the well. Only then the R-3LD flown by Kalyuzhnov landed nearby. While the commanders were yelling at each other, the *Basmachi* retreated safely. The air assault on the friendly unit was fortunately very ineffective: one squad leader and one horse were wounded. And this after a raid by almost the whole squadron! This fact casts considerable doubt on the triumphant reports of pilots about the complete defeat of entire enemy gangs.

The Khorezm group of Red Army troops – a motorised detachment of the OGPU and a Turkmen Cavalry Brigade – advanced towards the sands from the opposite side. They were supported first by three, then by nine reconnaissance aircraft and one transport Ju-13. The latter was soon out of action as while flying with passengers from Chardzhou to Novy Urgench, the plane of the 40th Air Unit (pilot N.M. Klochenko) broke the undercarriage strut during landing. The planned transportation of personnel was on the brink of failure, so another aircraft of the same type had to be leased from *Dobrolyot*.

The Khorezm group encountered no serious resistance. On 18 September the pilot Maltsev spotted an encampment in the Kesekli mountain area. The next day a unit of the OGPU arrived there. At dawn three R-3LDs of the 40th Air Unit bombed the encampment, the only gun of the OGPU unit fired a few shots, and then trucks with machine guns moved forward. The camp surrendered without a fight; the captives were numerous as about 20,000 people with lots of cattle were hiding in the area, with their camps stretching for 25–30km. The Red Army collected a large number of various weapons, but two gangs, totalling about 100 men, managed to escape.

Later, aviation was used mainly for reconnaissance and communications. There was one occasion when pilot Kalyuzhnov, Commander of the 35th Air Unit, went to look for an OGPU motorised unit. He flew for a long time and finally saw traces of the vehicles below. The pilot found the unit and dropped a message streamer with the order. Bombing missions were relatively rare – several missions were conducted near Tashauz. 'The work of aviation is faultless', reported the head of political department of the Turkmen Cavalry Brigade. However, by the end of September the entire Turkmen Air Group was already on the verge of losing combat effectiveness. The service life of the aircraft engines was almost exhausted as the pilots had flown twice as many hours as normal (according to the source from the 35th Air Unit, 'the usage of the airplanes was merciless'), the reserve of fuel was running out, and the crews were tired. Water, which was constantly in short supply, was the major challenge. Once, flasks with water were even collected from the ground crews to pour water into the aircraft radiators.

The hostilities continued, however, and the aviation was conducting intensive reconnaissance missions. Reports scrupulously listed the number of riders, yurts, camels and sheep that were spotted. From low altitudes the pilots searched for footprints and other traces on the sand, trying to determine where the enemy had gone. Thus, the report entry for 6 October says: 'Numerous traces were spotted near the Islam-kuyu Well'. Operations continued for almost another week, while on 12 October all aircraft departed to Tashkent, where they arrived three days later.

All the crews had accumulated many flying hours, as they spent six to eight hours a day in the air, and in some cases they flew up to three missions a day. In August–October alone, the aviators dropped 1,875 bombs and fired 25,883 shots. In total during the Kara-Kum campaign the aviation delivered 5,575kg of fuel and oil, 6,250kg of water, 1,320kg of food supplies, 1,650kg of fodder and 4,990kg of other cargoes. They transported 127 men of flight and ground crew and 187 servicemen of the Red Army and OGPU units. In one case, a machine-gun squadron with a light machine gun was transported. The work of the big ANT-9 was worthy of distinction: in two months, it transported 221 men (including 57 wounded) and 11,500kg of various cargoes, including fuel for aircraft and vehicles.

The only aircraft losses were due to accidents. There were four forced landings in the 37th Squadron alone. One accident can be attributed to commander's complacency and illiteracy – on 19 September 1931 pilot V.V. Vasilyev was flying R-3LD delivering the Chief of Staff of Khorezm group of troops Sokolov. The latter wanted to land in Kunya-Urgench. The airfield there was in a very poor condition, so the pilot tried to dissuade Sokolov, but the Chief of Staff gave a categorical order and did it in writing (apparently wrote it in pencil on a sheet of notebook). The outcome was a serious accident. The Chief of Staff of the 37th Squadron, A.R. Janko, however, was not killed in the crash. He was shot in the air while photographing the *Basmachi* camp near Lake Jamala. A few months earlier, an observer Balakirev had been wounded in the arm. The final report of the 16th Air Brigade says: 'The R-3LD aircraft are not suitable in operating under conditions of the district ...'. Its main disadvantage was a low service ceiling, making it difficult to fly in the mountains. The ANT-9 was positively marked, but its insufficient service ceiling was also noted.

In general, the 1931 campaign in Turkmenistan failed to achieve substantial results. The large gangs scattered into small groups and took refuge in the desert, and the number of enemies, perhaps, became even greater than before. Large gangs, supported by the population, continued to roam in the Kara-Kum Desert. The campaign officially ended in November 1931, and a wing of the 40th Air Unit was retained in the desert. However, its activities were limited to reconnaissance and show-of-strength flights.

14
THE YEAR OF 1932

The year of 1932 passed rather quietly on the whole – there were only occasional clashes with small *Basmachi* bands in the south. In January–February 1932 one wing (three airplanes) of the 40th Air Unit operated in this area and was actively used against the gangs of Durdy Murdy, Anna Kuli and Ahmet Bek.

The lull in the south made it possible to redeploy troops into northern Kazakhstan, where the locals dissatisfied with collectivisation gained support from across the Chinese border (the White Cossacks had settled there after the Civil War). Whereas in the south the *Basmachi* considered all Russians (and non-Muslims in general) enemies and even promoted the slogan 'For Soviets without Europeans!', in Kazakhstan the gangs consisted of mixed national groups and were often led by Russian officers. For example, one of the largest gangs was commanded by Colonel Polkovnikov. The fact is that in 1924 the Akmolinsk area had been transferred from Russian jurisdiction to Kazakhstan. This territory was populated by significantly more Russians than Kazakhs. Akmolinsk was later renamed numerous times – Tselinograd, Akmola, Astana – and is now called Nur-Sultan, which is the contemporary capital of Kazakhstan.

In April, the 37th Squadron and a wing from the 40th Air Unit were deployed to Kazakhstan, but the hostilities there did not last long – the Cossacks retreated across the Chinese border and were not pursued further. By the beginning of July the airplanes had returned to Tashkent.

By then almost all the R-3LDs of the Red Army Air Force were concentrated in Central Asia – in August 1932 there were 70 out of total 80, plus three older R-3M5s (powered by M-5 engines). This was due to the fact that the losses were compensated by the aircraft that became available after the conversion of air units in other districts. Those airplanes were badly deteriorated. The French Lorrain-Dietrich engines were repeatedly overhauled, and spare parts for them were in short supply. Twenty R-3LDs and two R-3M5s out of the aircraft available in the CAMD were listed as unserviceable. That is why the 16th Air Brigade began converting its units to new R-5 wooden biplanes. As mentioned above, the first

airplanes of this type arrived as early as 1931, and by the beginning of 1933 they accounted for more than half of the Brigade's fleet. However, the conversion process was delayed, as the *Basmachi* were not considered a serious adversary, so even outdated aircraft were good against them.

In addition to the R-3LD airplanes, the old R-3M5s powered by M-5 engines were sent to Central Asia from the central part of Russia to compensate for losses.

Crash of an R-3LD airplane *Komsomol Toçikiston* (*Young Communist League of Tajikistan*) flown by pilot V. Mareev from the 40th Air Unit in Tashkent, March 1932.

In Turkmenistan in 1932, unlike in the previous years, the troops were out in the field by the very end of autumn, and the scale of events was far less than in 1931. Hence, the aviation forces assigned to the troops were small – just one wing of the 1st Air Unit of the 37th Squadron and one wing of the 40th Air Unit were transferred from Tashkent. The opponents were the escaped gangs of Durdy Murdy, Anna Kuli and Ahmet Bek. The airplanes conducted reconnaissance, promptly dropping the message streamers with the results to the troops on the ground. For the first time, specially trained dogs were used to find and pick up the message streamers. Sometimes pilots themselves, in course of the reconnaissance, attacked the *Basmachi* with bombs and machine gun fire.

After the end of the 1931 campaign, the district command arrived at the conclusion that special air transport units should be

An R-3LD reconnaissance aircraft being repaired in the workshops of the 37th Aircraft Depot in Tashkent, 1932.

A border guard on duty in the mountains.

established. At the beginning of 1932 a squadron was formed – initially it was not a part of the regular unit, was called simply a Transport Squadron and operated the same heavily worn Ju-13s. Those aircraft proved to be durable, reliable and did not need high-quality landing grounds. Later, two R-3s and one R-5 aircraft were added to the fleet of the squadron, followed by the ANT-9, which previously belonged to the brigade command. The unit became designated as the 95th Separate Transport Squadron.

In June 1932 the squadron received a new eight-seat K-5 passenger airplane powered by an M-15 engine. Pilot S.M. Simachenko flew the K-5, which was used to carry both passengers and cargo. Somewhat later, the U-2 light biplanes powered by M-11 engine arrived and were employed as liaison aircraft, and in 1933 even a fighter was added to the Transport Squadron: this was an all-metal I-4 sesquiplane, which was then considered obsolete. As there was no air opponent for it in Central Asia, the command did not know where to put the fighter and assigned it to the transport unit.

The old Ju-13s still remained in service, although accidents were becoming more frequent. The already mentioned pilot Shnei was transporting ammunition from Ashgabat to the frontline site near Sernyi Zavod. In one of the flights he was caught in the fog, so he turned to low-altitude flying, but visibility was getting worse. Inevitably, he had had to land on the first more or less suitable ground. As the result, the airplane landing gear and propeller were damaged, but the pilot and the cargo-accompanying passenger

A K-5 passenger airplane; one such aircraft was used in the 95th Separate Transport Squadron.

One of the Ju-13s from the Transport Squadron placed on a flat car on the way to Tashkent for repairs, 1932.

as well as the cargo itself were intact, so they found them to be extremely lucky as the cargo was detonators for bombs.

By the end of January 1933, all aircraft involved in the operation were recalled. They were replaced by the airplanes of the 40th Air

Unit deployed in Kyzyl-Arvat. They operated in the Kara-Kum Desert until the end of March of the following year.

15
ESTABLISHING THE OGPU AVIATION

In 1932 a decree was issued on the establishment of the Border Guard Aviation, which was then under the jurisdiction of the OGPU. Among the first units to be formed were separate air units in Central Asia. The first to appear on 14 January 1932 was the 3rd Separate Air Unit in Alma-Ata, commanded by L. Vasilevskiy. Eight months later it was transferred to Burunday airfield, 18km from the city.

The 2nd Air Unit was established in Tashkent on 20 April 1932. In October 1933 it was transferred to Ashgabat and in May of the following year it was deployed to Merv (Mary). In Tashkent, in June 1932, it was replaced by the 1st Air Unit under the command of N. Zaborskiy. All those units were initially equipped with R-1 and R-3LD airplanes transferred from the Air Force, and according to the documents each unit was supposed to have 10 aircraft in its strength. In February 1933 the 4th Air Unit in Akmolinsk (commander K. Shishkov) was added. Border guards were charged with reconnaissance missions of frontier regions, communication

and, partly, transportation. They delivered mail, documents, weapons, ammunition and medications to commandant offices, outposts and frontier posts. The terrain conditions did not allow the border to be sealed off 'tightly', so the constant patrolling by aircraft significantly increased control over the adjacent areas.

From 1934 onwards, some of the air units were formed into bigger air squadrons. For instance, parts of three air units were united into the 3rd Air Squadron in Mary. The Air Squadron was supposed to have 31 aircraft in its strength. At the same time, the Border Guard pilots received new R-5 and U-2 biplanes.

The R-5 airplanes of the 1st Air Unit of the OGPU in Tashkent

In 1934, border guards operated one Sh-2 amphibian airplane, capable of landing both on land and water.

16
AT THE END OF THE LONG WAR

The obsolete R-3LDs were gradually being decommissioned, but those aircraft were still involved in operations of the following year. As of 1 January 1933, there were still 68 airplanes of this type in CAMD, 39 of which in serviceable condition. Such a low level of combat readiness vividly demonstrated the worn-out state of the aircraft after intensive operation under heavy conditions. On 19 January 1933 the commander of the CAMD forces reported to the Chairman of the Revolutionary Military Council of the USSR: 'The condition of R-3 airplanes with Lorraine-Dietrich engines operated by air units in the district entrusted to me is so poor due to the wear and tear, that it can provide combat readiness ... only for 1933'.

Crash of an R-5 flown by Wing Commander D.A. Barkov during military exercises in Samarkand, March 1934.

Crash of an R-5 airplane flown by pilot L.G. Petrushevskiy of the 37th Squadron, which happened when he attempted to take-off with the fuel pump turned off, August 1934.

The number of R-3LDs was gradually declining after accidents and crashes that were caused by the weather conditions, the difficulty of flying over mountains and deserts, unreliable equipment and, at times, simple carelessness. For instance, in June 1933 the unit commander V. V. Vasilyev got out of a plane without shutting down the engine, while the observer Kurnbaliev accidentally moved the throttle in the rear cockpit. The engine roared, and the R-3LD started to taxi along the airfield. Kurnbaliev, who did not know how to control the aircraft, panicked and jumped out of the plane. The uncontrolled biplane ran some distance around the airfield and then turned around on its own (apparently hitting a small obstacle), moved towards the parking line and damaged another R-3LD.

As of 1 March 1933, the CAMD had 67 R-3LDs, three R-3M5s, two R-5s and one I-4 aircraft in its strength. The R-5s also got into accidents – on 13 June 1933 the airplane of the same Commander of the 37th Squadron, Vasilyev, made a forced landing due to the engine failure. The arrival of the new R-5s created a surplus of aircraft in the brigade, so 10 R-3LDs were listed as stored in September 1933.

The fleet of the 16th Air Brigade was in almost the same condition at the end of 1933. The brigade had changed its designation by this time and

By the mid-1930s the TB-1 bomber had already become obsolete but was still quite suitable for use in Central Asia.

Border patrol in the mountains, 1937.

The final conversion of the entire 454th Air Brigade to R-5s was planned to be completed in 1934. However, by 1 January 1935 only the 37th Squadron had received a complete set of new aircraft (32 airplanes were at its disposal) and five more were listed in the 35th Air Unit. However, the task was completed eventually: by the end of February there were 52 R-5s in the Central Asian Military District. A year later, a TB-1 bomber unit was established in the district, which was mainly engaged in cargo transportation. The CAMD was considered secondary by the command as its neighbours, Iran and Afghanistan, did not have strong armies and their aviation was obsolete. Consequently, the aircraft fleet in the CAMD remained small and the operated types were obsolete.

was renamed into the 454th Mixed Air Brigade. From 1934 the troops were little involved in operations against the *Basmachi*. The main burden of activities fell on the units of the OGPU (it now became the part of NKVD, *Narodny Komissariat Vnutrennikh Del* – People's Commissariat for Internal Affairs, which by then had fully-operational aviation of its own). The R-5 airplanes, which were used by the NKVD air units, were employed both as transport and combat aircraft. The military were left with only occasional flights to assist the NKVD operations and the routine combat training.

However, the *Basmachi* did not disappear completely. Small gangs were still active – they periodically went abroad and then came back again. But the threat was no longer so serious that it called for using the army. The groups that had infiltrated across the border were successfully dealt with by border guards who had vehicles, motorbikes and airplanes. They also used horses that could go to the places where the wheels would fail, and the camels too. It seemed that the war in Central Asia had finally fallen into oblivion.

17
OPERATION IN XINJIANG

In July 1937 a rather large military operation was launched; officially it was called 'the struggle against the *Basmachi* in the Pamir Mountains'. However, it was actually an invasion into Chinese Xinjiang, where active hostilities were in process. Two divisions, one consisting of Dungans and the other of Uyghur, rioted against the *Duban* (governor) Sheng Shicai. They were supported by the locals (in Xinjiang the Chinese were a national minority).

The *Duban* had already established good relations with the USSR and in 1933–34, the Soviets secretly supported him against his rival, Ma Zhongying, and Muslim nationalists. In 1937 Sheng Shicai again asked his northern neighbour for help. Several regiments of the NKVD and the Red Army units equipped with artillery and armoured vehicles were deployed across the border. They were supported by an air group of 25 to 35 aircraft.

The core of the group was about 30 R-5 airplanes of the Border Guard forces. They were gathered from the 1st (based in Bykovo near Moscow), 3rd (from Alma-Ata) and 4th (Mary) Air Squadrons and concentrated at Turugard airfield on the border between Kazakhstan and China. The temporary unit was commanded by Captain I. Chuprov. In addition, three (according to other sources, five) TB-3RN bombers were added to the group, manned by the crews from the brigade stationed in Rostov-on-Don.

The R-5 aircraft of the border guards were conducting reconnaissance missions, sometimes combining them with air strikes on identified enemy troops. For instance, Chuprov's crew once spotted a group of soldiers in a campsite, dropped bombs and fired machine guns at them. In addition, the airplanes occasionally supported attacks of friendly troops on the ground. Pilots Stepanov, Kirzhak and Yevdokimov were regularly engaged in assaulting ground targets. The R-5s also carried documents, weapons, ammunition, food and medical supplies. They were also used for urgent delivery of commanders and specialists to the battle sites. The R-5 flown by Yevdokimov was hit during a combat mission, the aircraft caught fire and crashed, the crew were killed. The other aircraft of the group also sustained battle damages during combat operations.

The TB-3RN bombers were first transferred to an intermediate site on the Soviet side of the border, near a border outpost at 3,000m above sea level. The runway there had to be lengthened to allow take-off of the fully-loaded bombers which carried ammunition and fuel for armoured vehicles. While landing in China, the TB-3RN

piloted by N. Sushin rolled out into a ditch and caught fire. The crew were not injured but the aircraft had to be written off. The bombers alternated between bombing missions and transporting men and cargo. During one of the bombing raids the airplane piloted by Pleshakov was hit and the crew were killed in a crash.

The flights were challenged by difficult mountain conditions, dust storms and poorly equipped temporary airfields. In one case, pilot Trigidko and his crew lost their bearings, ran out of fuel and made a forced landing in a mountain valley near a river. The crew of another airplane, flown by F.N. Orlov, spotted them and the pilot was able to land on the other bank of the river. For two days the two crews cleared rocks, preparing the runways for take-off, and carried buckets of fuel across the river. As a result of their efforts, both TB-3RNs managed to take-off successfully.

The insurgents maintained ties with the Japanese, so there were several Japanese air raids on airfields and troop deployments. The bomber piloted by the same Orlov was engaged in a special mission to capture the commander of one of the rebel divisions. A Japanese aircraft was supposed to be flown to Khotan airfield for this commander, but a repainted TB-3RN arrived instead. The crew took the general and his escort aboard and delivered them straight into enemy hands.

The flights in Xinjiang were completed by the end of October 1937, and in January of the following year the Soviet troops withdrew from the Chinese territory. The Border Guard airplanes returned to their permanent deployment areas, and the TB-3RNs were ferried to Poltava.

18
IN THE EARLY 1940s

In 1938 Soviet air units in Central Asia, along with other units of the Air Force, switched to a regimental structure. A standard air regiment consisted of five squadrons of 12 aircraft each plus three airplanes in the command wing: a total of 63 aircraft. The fleet of the regiments was supplemented with more advanced aircraft types.

As of 20 September 1940, the Air Force of CAMD had the following types in its strength: 15 TB-3 heavy bombers, six old TB-1 bombers, 72 SB high-speed bombers, 19 R-5 reconnaissance and liaison aircraft, 12 R-Zet light bombers (wooden biplanes powered by M-34NB engines) and 69 DI-6 two-seat fighters which were also used for ground-attack roles. The district also had a full-fledged fighter aviation, operating I-16 monoplanes.

The aircraft fleet of the Border Troops was also upgrading gradually. However, they continued to receive the types that were written off from the Air Force arsenal. Thus they received R-10 reconnaissance monoplanes and SB bombers which allowed to the Border Guard forces to conduct regular patrol flights of the border regions.

On the morning of 22 June 1941 Germany attacked the USSR. In August of the same year, fearing an increase of the German influence in a strategically important country, the Soviet Union and Britain

DI-6 two-seat fighters were often used for ground-attack roles.

An R-10 reconnaissance monoplane; such aircraft were transferred from the Air Force to the Border Guard aviation in the late 1930s.

The SB high-speed bomber was the most advanced aircraft in Central Asia in the late 1930s.

occupied Iran – the British moved from the south, the Soviets from the north. Military units from the CAMD were also engaged – the 53rd Separate Army, supported by aviation, advanced from Turkmenistan. The main role was played by the 1st High-speed Bomber Regiment which operated SB airplanes. The resistance of the Iranians was weak, so bombing was carried out only during the first days, and then the missions were limited to reconnaissance and dropping leaflets.

After the German invasion of the USSR, the *Basmachi* who had settled in Afghanistan resumed active operations. By then they had already established ties with German intelligence, which began to finance them. Starting from July, some groups began preparations to return to the Soviet territory. The rapid advance of the Germans gave them obvious enthusiasm, and they assumed that the Soviet command would withdraw either all or at least the majority of the troops from Central Asia, so the remaining units and the border guards would not be able to withhold a large grouping of forces. Indeed, the 1st High-speed Bomber Regiment was directed to the front in October 1941 and took part in the Battle of Moscow.

The previously mentioned Kurshermat still nurtured the hope of restoring the Emirate of Bukhara. A group of Afghan leaders led by the Crown Prince thought of annexing Bukhara and Khorezm to Afghanistan, and the Afghan Emir even made a secret agreement with the former Emir of Bukhara Seyyid Alim Khan. They thought that one division of the Afghan army combined with several

thousand *Basmachi* would be enough to seize those cities. Some former *kurbashi* claimed that they could quickly gather up to 40,000 men. Such numbers were doubtful, of course, but the Germans were constantly given inflated figures in order to extract more money from them.

The operation was expected to begin after the German forces had taken Moscow and Leningrad. Soviet intelligence had information on Afghan and *Basmachi* plans, so the preparations were made to 'greet the guests'. The Air Force of the CAMD was also being prepared.

However, near the Soviet capital the Hitler's army got his first big kick and rolled backwards. Under pressure from the British, the Afghans arrested Kurshermat in May 1942, which became another blow to the grand idea. The hopes of the *Basmachi* were revived when, after an unsuccessful Red Army offensive near Kharkov in the summer of 1942, the German troops advanced towards the Volga. However, this ended in the defeat of the 6th Army of Field Marshal Paulus, which surrendered in the ruined city of Stalingrad.

After that, the plans of invading Soviet Central Asia were no longer discussed. The unconquered *Basmachi* stayed in Afghanistan, looking for patrons. Some began to work for German, Turkish, British and even Japanese intelligence, and their masters sent them in search of the information into the Soviet territory. However, these were only the occasional border trespassers, and they were hunted down by border guards and Soviet counter-intelligence. The *Basmachi* movement faded away.

BIBLIOGRAPHY

Dyomin, A.A., *Aviatsiya velikogo soseda* (Moscow: Russkiye Vityazi, 2008)

Eliseev, S.P., *Organizatsionnoye stroitelstvo sovetskikh Voyenno-vozdushnykh Sil (1921–1931)* (Moscow: VVA, 2012)

Konev V.N., Zinoviev N.N., *Krasniye aviatory na frontakh grazhdanskoy voiny* (Moscow: Russkiye Vityazi, 2018)

Konev, V.N., Zinoviev, N.N., *Krasniye aviatory v nebe 1920-kh godov* (Moscow: Russkiye Vityazi, 2018)

Krasniy vozdushniy flot 1918–1923 (Moscow: 1924)

Krasniy vozdushniy flot na sluzhbe revolyutsii. Boyeviye epizody (Moscow: Voyennyi Vestnik, 1923)

Krylatoye plemya (Moscow: Voenizdat, 1962)

Lebedev, A.A., Mazuruk, I.P., *Nad Arktikoy i Antarktikoy* (Moscow: Mysl, 1991)

Tumanskiy, A.K., *Polyot skvoz gody* (Moscow: Voenizdat, 1962)

Magazines
Aviatsia I Khimiya
Aero
Vestnik Vosdushnogo Flota
Grazhdanskaya Aviatsiya
Dayesh Motor
Samolyot
Khronika Vozdushnogo Dela

Archives
Central House of Aviation and Cosmonautics
Russian State Archive of Economics
Russian State Archive of Social and Political History
Russian State Military Archive
Scientific and Memorial Museum of N.E. Zhukovskiy

Photos
Photos are courtesy of the above archives, as well as from the personal archives of the author and Gennady Petrov.

ABOUT THE AUTHOR

Vladimir Kotelnikov was born in Moscow on 9 December 1951. He graduated from the Moscow Aviation Institute (University) in 1975 and was engaged in research and development in the area of high-temperature strength, defended the academic degree of the Candidate of Science in 1981 and read lectures on aircraft piston engine design at Moscow Aviation Institute.

From the 1980s Kotelnikov conducted archive research on the history of Russian aviation of the inter-war and Second World War period. As the result of his work, he published several hundred articles and dozens of books in Russia and abroad, among them – *British and American Aircraft in Russia prior to 1941*, *Lend-Lease and Soviet Aviation*, *Russian Piston Aero Engines*, *Air War Over Khalkhin Gol*, *Petlyakov Pe-2* and others.

Being an aviation historian, Vladimir received a diploma of a professor of the Academy of Aviation and Aeronautics Science and acted as consultant on piston aero engines design to Russian aviation museums and aircraft restoration groups.

Vladimir Kotelnikov passed away in August 2022.